13 Key Strategies to Make Money Fast in Business

Stephen Paluszek

In Collaboration with Twelve World Entrepreneurs

Publishing History

Paperback Edition 1 / October 2019
ISBN-13: 9781701917095

Dedication

"To my parents, for always believing in me and encouraging me to chase my dreams." – Stephen Paluszek

"To my husband Rizal for believing in me and for letting me fly high. To Ba and Yaya, Mommy loves you so much! To my family for your unconditional love and support." – Dr. Izdihar Jamil

"To my wife, Kristen for unconditional love and support along this bumpy journey." – Amanda Rush

"For the women who were told they shouldn't, couldn't or wouldn't. Your dreams deserve to be felt by those who doubt you. Create a business that leaves a legacy and transforms lives. To become an ICON, affirm: I CAN!" – Arooj Ashraf

"I'm dedicating this book to everyone who's working hard for their "Big Whys". Thank you to my family and friends for their love and support" – Azlin Ishak, Malaysia

"To my late dad, you are the successful businessman. The world knows your story. To my mom thank you for believing in me. To my husband, I am grateful to have you." – Dr. Hanim Romainoor.

"To all those who love someone and would like to change their life to be better. To my family & Eesa- I love you all so much and thank you for believing in me." – Ija Juhari

"I dedicated myself to life long learning, sharing knowledge unconditionally and making people feel better than they did before meeting me." – Nikoleta Djordjevic

"I dedicate this book to my beloved family. Without their unconditional support and love I would not have achieved what I have today. I would also like to thank the parents and coaches of my talents for believing in me and entrusting me to develop their children. I also thank all the talents I've had a chance to work with. I hope you would all continue to achieve success in your chosen sports." – Dato' Sayed Al Feizal & Datin Shomiriza Shomidon

"To my late father, Ayah, I miss you. To my mum, Ummi and mum in-law Mummy, I love you. To my Mr Pilot, Captain Zam Zam Abu Hassan, thank you for your unconditional love. Family & Friends, my heartfelt gratitude" – Dr. Sawiah Jusoh

"To all the generous souls who have impacted upon my life in a beautiful way – whether you knew it at the time or not. Thank you for being all that you are." – Silas J. Lees

"To my loving parents, brother and sister, for their relentless support on the journey. I love you all!" – Tyson Sharpe

"I would like to dedicate this chapter to my beloved husband, children, family, close friends and everyone who endlessly giving me courage and motivation to contribute to the ummah. May Allah bless all of us and place us in the Jannatul Firdaus." – Yentti Amir

Reviews

"Dr. Izdihar Jamil is one of the most influential, pure hearted and exceptional individuals I have had the pleasure to meet. What makes her so successful in business is that "she is her product"! When people buy you first, what you're offering them after that is a direct result of them feeling an honest connection with you. From her joyful spirit to her contagious energy for life. When you experience her methods and coaching strategies for business. You will discover why not only this book is a must have, but she is a much needed strategist in today's business culture." – Jairrod A. Burch, Expert Value Empowerment Speaker/CEO/Author/ Influencer & Value Life Coach Specialist

"A superb compilation of real life stories from Entrepreneurs who have used their personal and business adversities to build highly successful businesses. I really enjoyed reading it and have picked up some great ideas to implement into my business."
– Audra Starkey, Nutritionist and Author of *Too Tired To Cook*.

"This book gave me motivation and ideas on how to grow my momprenuer business." – Breshna Hazrat, Mompreneur, USA

"From time to time you get a coach come forward that is truly thankful and helpful at the same time. That said, this lady is here to get you results – results in leads, results in sales, and results which will enable you to build a real business. This is a great and simple read to spark action in your business. Izdihar, you are a star!" – Linda Morrison, Online Business Coach, Australia

Table of Contents

Introduction

This book shares the inspiring stories of 13 successful Entrepreneurs from around the world as they share the key strategies that they used to make money fast in their business.

Each strategy is unique to each author as they take you on their journey. You'll come to see that life isn't just about unicorn and roses. Behind every success there are untold stories- the challenges, the fear, the breakdowns and the miracles.

Collectively the key strategies are powerful methods for anybody to be successful in both business and personal. Apply them to your life and you'll start to see changes and transformation.

The Entrepreneurs are real people just like you who has big dreams. They are real people with real results- they are not fictional characters. What makes them extraordinary are their faith and the actions that they took to make the impossible possible.

We hope you'll enjoy reading this book as much as we have loved sharing our stories with you.

Miracles happen to ordinary people who makes extraordinary choices and actions every day. You have what it takes to be successful. You just have to believe in yourself and make things happen.

You and your family deserve the best possible future. Go for it, it is yours!

> *"There are only two ways to live your life. One is as though nothing is a miracle. The other is as though everything is a miracle."*
> – Albert Einstein

Love, light and joy,

Stephen

Izdihar

Amanda

Arooj

Azlin

Hanim

Ija

Nikoleta

Sawiah

Sayed & Shomi

Silas

Tyson

Yentti

13 Key Strategies to Make Money Fast in Business

Stephen Paluszek

Consistency

By Stephen Paluszek
Real Estate Productivity Coach, USA

"We are what we repeatedly do excellence, therefore is not an act but a habit" –
Aristotle

The Backstory

Growing up in Philadelphia, Pennsylvania in a hard-working family, I always knew the value of showing up. My parents would never worry much about my grades, but as long as I showed up to school every single day, that is what mattered most to them. They emphasized that being consistent every day was the most important thing. This was a lesson that would be instilled in me, and that has nurtured me throughout my journey in life.

The Drama

As far back as I can remember, I have always wanted to be an entrepreneur. I would see people driving to work every day and knew this lifestyle would never much appeal to me. Many of you that have taken this journey can relate – knowing you want something different in life, but not being sure how to get it.

My journey took me down so many different paths; the best way I could describe my emotions is I just felt lost. I knew I wanted to do something, but I had a lot of uncertainty on what the action should be. This took me on an adventure, even traveling the world, just to figure it out.

My goal was to find what I really wanted in life. I tried everything over this time period. I began teaching classes at the gym, learning computer programming, working in property management, and investing in real estate. I was essentially doing a little bit of everything.

The problem was nothing ever seemed to stick. I would easily get excited about an idea and start off with a lot of "motivation," yet before I knew it, my motivation would fade. I always felt like I was just going back to the starting point over and over again. This left me feeling confused. How could I be so excited about an idea but not have enough follow-through to stick with it?

The Turning Point

At some point, I realized my situation had to change. I found myself 27 years old, living in Las Vegas, and still "looking" endlessly for what I wanted to do in life. I sat up late one night and thought to myself, "*This is not the life I want to be living.*" I finally made the choice to stop running on the hamster wheel and actually make a real change. This emotional low point is what encouraged me to obtain a productivity coach, a decision that caused everything to change.

As I started to really step back to look at myself in the third person and not keep looking at myself from my own point of view, I started to think long term. What do I want in five years, 10 years, or 20 years – not just in the next five minutes or even today? This new mentality changed my perspective completely. It made me see that what I was doing now was not supporting me in the long term. It wasn't going to get me where I am now to where I wanted to go.

This is something I highly recommended if you are not fully satisfied with how things are going in your life. Start to envision and really think how you would love to see your life one year, five years, or 10 years from now. Then, start reverse-engineering your life. We are creatures of habit, and chances are things will stay the same if you don't make a conscious effort to change.

One of my favorite metaphors of this is thinking about oneself as a ship setting out to sea with no destination or goal. Let's say you head out of New York in your ship with no destination. You are going to head into the Atlantic Ocean, yet after a few days as you drift away from land, you will feel extremely lost. You will be floating aimlessly with pretty much two destinations to arrive at. The first is you will decide to turn around and go back where you started. The second is you will just drift until you end up in a place you didn't even choose.

Now, let's take a ship with a goal and a map or GPS. Say the goal is to arrive in Europe. You head out of New York, and your voyage will invariably get difficult. You may have bad weather on top of many other challenges, yet deep down you will have the calm, confident attitude that you will arrive at your destination. Why? Because you have not only the goal but the tools to help guide you there. This is exactly the same when it comes to our lives. First, you must see your destination or goal and start working toward it. If you continue to sail as in the second scenario described above, you will continue to drift around with no destination or overall purpose.

The Vision

I applied this scenario to my life. I was drifting for 27 years, never thinking about the future. I was sailing my ship aimlessly and never building a map or knowing the destination I wanted to reach. The big question I finally asked myself was, *"What do I really want?"* This is not what I think I want, not what others want for me. It is simply, *"What do I really want?"* This question changed my life. I took some self-analysis, like *"What am I good at and love to do?"* and *"What is one thing I could do every day for the rest of my life?"*

I knew it wasn't working in an office. I loved interacting with people and seeing what makes them happy. I've always loved helping people. I knew if I could help people every day, I would feel fulfilled. I finally made the decision. I knew now what I was going to do, and I committed myself to it.

Having a coach to ask me these questions and take me through this process had changed my life tremendously. I felt like a new person – much more relaxed, focused, successful, and happy. I knew I had to give this gift to others, but how?

I built the vision in my mind first. I could see myself coaching others to succeed in their lives. I could see myself living in beautiful southern California connecting with people from all over the world through my computer screen. I committed myself by reading every book I could on the subject, attending seminars, and buying the best online programs.

The Call to Action

As much as I wanted to help everyone, I quickly realized the person who helps everyone helps no one. I tried to think more about who really needed help. What group of people was there that needed help that I could connect with and relate with? I thought back to my previous experiences and what I had learned. One of the biggest fields of need I could see was in real estate.

First, this was a business I had been involved in for many years. During my time working in real estate offices, property management, and investing, I had seen a lot. The unfortunate reality is that most people do not view real estate agents in the most positive light. I knew agents personally, and they loved their job and helping people with real estate transactions. Another unfortunate fact is the high fail-out rate of real estate agents. It's estimated that 87% of them fail within five years of being in the business. That means only about 10% succeed, and the top one or two percent make most of the money. I thought to myself, *How is this possible? How can this high percentile of good people fail?*

I made a decision that I would do my best to help change this.

As I started to study this field, I understood there had to be something 10% of the agents do that 90% fail to do. I heard a quote once, and I absolutely loved it. It is *"Success leaves clues."* No matter what you are trying to succeed in, there are clues. Someone before you has done it. You need to go to them and learn exactly what they have done and copy their successful methods. If you try to do and learn everything on your own, this will only lead to frustration and anxiety. In real estate, the average realtor only does one to two transactions a year! This only brings $5,000 to $30,00 a year in commissions before taxes. Once I had seen this, I set out to build a simple, step-by-step process to help realtors build the life and business of their dreams.

The Downfall

I was fired up! I spent numerous hours and days pursuing my goal of building the best realtor-coaching program I could. I thought about their pains and their desires, the things they were doing right and the things they were doing wrong. I realized that everyone is different; therefore, I made this program something that could work for anyone – male or female, new or experienced. I was finally all set and ready to go to market. After some ups and downs, I began to get traction. I started to get attention and attract clients. Things began rolling, but something was missing.

Things just felt a little unpredictable. I started to get results one week, and then the next week, nothing. I felt like I was just going on an unpredictable roller-coaster ride. Can you relate to this? You tell yourself you're going to start something new. Maybe it's going to the gym, cutting out bad foods, or even starting your own business. You feel excited, motivated. You feel ready to go. You tell yourself this is it, no more "everything changes" now. Then, before you know it, you just don't stick to it. You may self-sabotage or whatever you want to call it. This is exactly what happened to me on that roller coaster of unpredictability in my life and business. This caused me massive frustration, and I truly didn't know what was wrong.

The Key Ingredient

I tried the best I could to step back into the third person and look at my business and myself. So many different thoughts came flooding in – *What could it be? Is it my marketing? Is it my program?* I started to look at everything outside myself. It was almost like I was looking for something or someone to blame. I realized I was always looking <u>outside</u> myself and not <u>at</u> myself. One day, a light bulb went off one word came to my mind. It all had to do with – <u>consistency</u>!

Consistency, I thought. Could it really be that simple? *No way!* I thought it had to be something "bigger and badder" than just simple consistency.

I thought about everything in life and in the world, and I realized consistency is key for success in anything. If you have a plant at home, you need to water it consistently, or it dies. We need to do maintenance to our house or car, or they will fall apart. Similarly with our bodies, we need to exercise consistently to maintain a healthy lifestyle. We need to eat healthy consistently to feel the way we really want to. If any of these are neglected, we fall apart or break down, and it is the exact same with business.

As I was coaching, I could see this was also a problem with many of my clients. In real estate, there are many different ways you can go about increasing your income. Sometimes we may think that increase in income is going to come to us through the latest technology. In today's world, we always seem to be thinking the latest app is going to be the next big thing that takes us over the top. Every day, it seems there is a new app that promises to be the solution to our problems.

What I found was truly amazing was my clients who took consistent action every day had ten times the results over those who could not stay consistent. Although some strategies are better than others in real estate success, consistency topped them all. A client who may not have the best strategy at first but stayed consistent every single day, would dominate over others who may have had more tools but did not take action every day. I couldn't believe that what seems like such a simple step to most, consistency, could be one of the biggest factors when it comes to success.

The Growth

Could this be one of the key ingredients to my program? I thought to myself. As a result of using some of the best real estate strategies and implementing consistent action in both my clients and myself, everything changed. I started building my business. Clients started to close more deals and everything flowed.

That was it! Helping realtors to build higher-quality leads, close more deals, and increase their income through my "6 Figure Realtors System", I stayed consistent reaching out every single day to new clients, getting on sales calls, offering free training – all while staying on top of investing and learning from the best in the real estate and success game.

By focusing-in on giving my clients a proven step-by-step process to achieve their real estate goals as quickly as possible, my 6 Figure Realtors Program was a success! My clients loved it!

The Reward

This is just the beginning of my life-long journey. Thinking back to being in Las Vegas just a short time ago to now living in southern California, living by the beach, and doing what I love, I can only be grateful for all the things that have come into my life.

The Brightness of the Future

I am currently scaling up my business and helping realtors from all across the country increase their income. Every single day, I am working to make the 6 Figure Realtors Program the best real estate program on the market today. On top of that, I am working to be the best coach in the world so I can inspire others to change their lives to give them the opportunity to live the life they have always dreamed of.

The Wisdom

Knowing what I know now, if there is just one piece of advice that I can share with you to bring you success in your life and business, it would be to believe in yourself and your vision and take <u>consistent</u> action every day.

Remember the metaphor of you as a ship. You always start off with your goal, your vision, the right tools, and the knowledge of the destination where you want to end up. We never know exactly how long our journey will take. I could take weeks, months, or even years. You may even get lost at sea. All that matters is you take consistent action every day and know your vision. Although some days may be tougher than others. before you know it. you will arrive at the destination of your dreams. Always remember, "<u>Consistency</u> is key."

Success Actions

Here are three success actions that you can take right now to make things happen in your business:

1. Have a clearly defined vision of what results you want to achieve in your life and business;
2. Believe in your ability to overcome anything that may get in your way;
3. Take one step every single – and be consistent!

Go out and live the life you deserve,

Stephen Paluszek

About the Author

Stephen Paluszek,
Real Estate productivity Coach, USA

Stephen Paluszek was born and raised in Philadelphia, Pennsylvania. He currently resides in sunny southern California. Stephen is a real estate productivity coach who helps his clients change their life and business through his "6 Figure Realtors System". He loves to help his clients build the life of which they have always dreamed.

Contacts

- **Business Name:** Paluszek Consulting
- **Website:** www.stephenpaluszek.com
- **Email:** stephen@stephenpaluszek.com
- **Facebook:** Stephen Paluszek
- **Linkedin:** Stephen Paluszek
- **Products/Services:** 6 Figure Realtors Program
- **Ideal Clients:** I specialize in working with real estate agents who are looking to scale to 6 figures and above.

- **Facebook Page for All Readers and Fans:** (Tips, Strategies, Ideas, Inspiring Stories to Make Money Fast In Business) https://www.facebook.com/groups/makemoneyfastinbusiness/, or search for "Make Money Fast in Business"

It's All about the Market

By Dr. Izdihar Jamil
Money Coach & Consultant, USA

"Success doesn't happen to you. It happens because of you!" ~ Grant Cardone

The Ordinary World

As the eldest of four girls (yes, four girls under one roof!), I always remembered growing up in Malaysia enjoying a happy childhood. Though we may be labeled as a Third World country with backward traditions, what I saw and experienced were joy, laughter, and delicious food!

My parents are hard-working professionals – my dad works in IT, and my mom was a chemistry teacher. My sisters and I were raised to be respectful, work hard in our studies, and have strong family values. One of my happiest memories is when family members gathered in my mom's living room after delicious meals. The laughter, the warmth, and the love were pure joy.

After college, I got married to an amazing guy and moved to England where he worked. I continued with my study, worked, and then completed my Ph.D. in

Computer Science. We are blessed with two children – a boy and a girl. One day, my husband said, *"What do think about moving to America? I've got a job offer!"* It was his dream job. Well, who am I to stand between a man and his dream, right? So, we packed up our life and moved to America.

This all sounds like a fairy tale come true story, right? Well, my friends, you're in for a ride because life isn't just all unicorns and roses!

The Drama

"We are here!" my little heart whispered when we arrived in America. I grew up watching Hollywood movies, saw all the glitter, and heard all the stories about how anything is possible in America. My parents, a few of my aunties and uncles, studied in America, and they always shared their experiences here with me. In a way, I had such an excellent impression of America even before coming here. Little did I know that I was opening up my family to a world of harassment and abuse just because we are Muslim and I wear the hijab. People called me vicious names in front of my children. It was a good thing that they were young then and weren't permanently affected by those incidents. I was harassed at the grocery store. One time, a guy came up to me and asked if I would do horrible things to people. I told him, *"I'm a mom myself. I wouldn't do that to anybody!"* He then asked, *"But if you were not a mom, would you do it?"* God, how could anyone think I could do those despicable things!

I had shit (literally!) threw onto our front door. My kids asked me, *"Why did they do that, Mommy?"* How can any mom answer questions like that without falling to pieces? Somehow, I gathered my strength and said, "*It's because they didn't make good choices.*"

We had police knocking at our door at midnight and accusing us of doing appalling things. They wouldn't even listen to what we said and came with biased judgments and preconceptions. I was trembling. I could feel anxiety creeping all over me. I couldn't sleep. I couldn't breathe. It was utterly horrible!

I've never been treated so awfully in my life before. Just because we choose to believe what we choose to believe, people automatically think that we're bad people who would do despicable things. Yes, we are Muslims, born and raised. Yes, there are crazy people out there who claimed to do horrible things in the name of religion. But they are not us or even close to representing the 1 billion Muslims around the world. Being judged by our appearance weren't allowed to show our true selves to people .

My core beliefs are based on the way I was raised by amazing parents who taught me to be kind, respectful, responsible, hardworking, and helpful to people. I love my family, and they love me. I work hard at school and in my career. I love food, and many times have cooked a nice meal for my neighbors and friends. I teach my kids the same principles and values, and I do not tolerate anything less. So, how are we so different from other families?

I had no close family in America. I didn't know whom I could ask for help. I was sad all the time. There were days when I cried and cried and cried. I didn't feel safe going out. I didn't feel safe taking my kids out with me. At times, I felt that I'd made the biggest mistake of my life in coming to America. I felt like the worst mom in the world having the audacity to expose my kids to such danger.

I knew I couldn't live like this anymore. It was eating me alive. I was like a zombie walking around. How could I get up from this? How could I be free from this?

The Turning Point

One night I was reading a storybook to my children at their bedtime. It was our typical bedtime routine. I asked my kids to choose a book, and they did. I turned to the chapter that they wanted and started reading the story. It was about a group of young men who ran away from a tyrant for fear that they would be killed for practicing their beliefs. They were faced with great difficulties and were fighting for their lives.

As I was reading the story, I came across this line: *"Ask for His Mercy and Help, and you shall receive it!"*. I couldn't believe it! It was like I was given the keys to the kingdom! I read the lines again and again. A wave of emotions came flowing over me – sadness, curiosity, relief, joy, and happiness. I started to feel lighter. It was like a huge weight was lifted off me. In my heart, I believe that the Creator Himself was speaking to me and offering me His Help and Mercy.

Every day I asked for God's Help and Mercy. I stopped playing the "victim" (clearly that hadn't done me much good!) and took charge of my life. I started to focus on the good things and the blessings that I have. I am what I tell myself to be. Every day I choose to be happy, courageous, kind, and loving.

Somehow, from that moment on, things started to get better and better. The harassment stopped. I felt safer. I was happier. I'm smiling more. Just the other day when I went shopping, a guy came up to us and said, *"Ma'am, I like your hijab, and you have every right to be in this country!"* Awwww! What amazing words to make someone feel appreciated, right? *"Thank you. I really appreciate it!"* I said with a big smile.

How was this shift happening, you may ask. I guess it started the moment I choose to ask the Creator to help me, like going back to the Source. It was also the moment that I started to choose whom I get to be every moment. I'm done with reacting, being a victim, and playing the blame game. I choose to be a powerful creator in my life. I choose happiness and goodness, no matter what!

Pondering upon this blessing (yes – that's how I choose to see it!), I feel that there was a message for me. I feel like no other families should go through what I went through. I feel like I should be a light to other families and help them to have the best possible future, to help them feel safe and happy, because isn't that what everybody deserves?

The Vision

I knew I wanted to help people. I knew that I was meant for something big in life. After making the choice to leave a prominent position to follow my husband to America and also to look after my kids, I knew that I was more than just a stay-at-home mom. But what was it?

With a Ph.D. and solid work experience, I could easily go back to working in a corporation or academia. My husband and I owned a successful, organic delivery business which delivered organic meat and poultry from the farm directly to our customers' doors. So, creating another business was a possibility, but I didn't want to be physically attached to a location while running the business.

So, the question that kept lingering in my mind was how could I use my skills and expertise and still nurture my family. How can I have both a successful career and family without compromise?

One day my husband told me, *"I bought a program from this coach so you can work from anywhere!"* The program was about how to become a successful online consultant and coach. The idea was that with a laptop and access to Wi-Fi, anyone could run his or her business from anywhere. The idea intrigued me because I could immediately envision myself running an online business while nurturing my family.

Since then, my husband kept on asking me, *"Have you started the program yet?"* At some point, I got annoyed with him asking me that question again and again. I started the program just to get him off my back.

My husband saw a vision of me working from anywhere around the world while taking care of my family and having the best of both worlds! What a blessing it is to have your other half have so much faith in you and encourage you toward something amazing.

The Call to Action

I spend months learning about how to become an online consultant and coach. My previous experience of having a business helped to shape things up and fuel my confidence. One of the first things I did was to understand the market. What does the market want? What kinds of problems or pains do they have? What are their challenges? What is the outcome that they want to achieve? What I know is that *"We can only sell what the market wants."*

So, even before designing a solution for my prospective customers, I needed to find out what that solution will help them to solve. But where do I start? Whom should I ask? What questions should I ask? I started to choose a niche, a small section of the market. If you try to catch everything, you'll catch nothing, so, I needed to narrow things down and be focused.

I looked at my passions and what I'm good at. I'm passionate about moms (because I'm a mom myself!) and I love money (who doesn't, right?). As a result of various training and seminars that I've taken, I'm very good at managing money. *"Maybe I can ask moms to see if they need help to manage and save money,"* I thought to myself. What have I got to lose, right?

I started talking to my friends who are moms to explore this topic further. I find this to be the most effective way to find out exactly what they need. After many conversations, the moms indicated they wanted help to take control of their finances, save money, be debt free fast, and have a solid nest egg for the future.

"I know how to solve that problem!" I excitedly thought to myself. I was in the same position as those moms years ago. I've got a great system that could really help that niche. I'm excited!

The Downfall

When I was in Montreal, Canada to present my Ph.D. work at a prestigious conference, I started to develop my "Diamond Queen Savings Program" (it's now known as the "6-Figure Savings System") to help moms take control of their finances and be debt free fast. Let's just say that I was inspired to start things there because it after six years of rejection, my paper was accepted, and there I was proudly presenting my work on stage in front of the world's best. In a way, it showed me that success is about persistence, consistency, and commitment.

So, I put together a 10-week program for the moms. I spent weeks refining the program because I wanted to include everything that I've learned that could help the moms and their finances. I thought it was epic – my best work ever! I was really excited to share it with the world and help make a huge difference to families everywhere.

When it was ready, I started to ask around if anybody would be interested in the program. I sent messages to my personal contacts, put a post on Facebook, and asked my friends. With that effort. I got a few calls which I was really excited about. The feedback I got was that my program seemed to be a good fit to help solve their problem. But when I asked, *"Do you want to join the program?"* they all said *"No."* I got really frustrated. I knew I had something great, but they are not biting. I'm hitting a brick wall, here! What was missing?

As I listened to the feedback from my niche, there were two major roadblocks – money and timeframe. As most of them are having financial struggles, they didn't have the money to pay for the program. The timeframe was also a challenge because when I mentioned 10 weeks, I could hear resistance. *"Huh? Did you say 10 weeks? Hmmm ..."*

"Okay," I thought, *"how can I make this work? I know this is what they want, so how can I make it irresistible?"* I asked myself.

The Key Ingredients

My niche was stressed out with their finances, so 10 weeks is too long for them to wait for results. I needed to shorten the time. With their financial struggles, I also needed to tweak my fee so that it was more affordable, something they could to jump right into without breaking their bank accounts.

With this feedback, I completely re-designed my offer and kept testing the market. When I received feedback, I tweaked it and tested it again. This was an iterative loop that I kept applying until the no's became yes's! I mean, you can only sell what the market wants, right?

My previous offer was 10 weeks for $2,500 for the Money Savings Program. My new offer was now 7 days for $497. What I offered them was a system that can help them take control of their finances and consistently save money. It sold the Program <u>multiple</u> times because it's <u>exactly</u> what the market wants! My best friend was one of my first paying clients followed by many women and men from all around the world. What a blessing!

The Growth

"Why don't you teach people how to make money too?" my coach asked me one day. When he asked that, I could feel my insecurities and doubt creeping in. *"But I don't know how to do it! I'm not good enough! I'm just good at teaching people to <u>save</u> money!"* my little

voice whispered. It took me awhile to digest his suggestion and see it from a different perspective.

Then one day I thought, *"Why not? What have I got to lose? I'm blessed to be making money in my business. I've learned tons of strategies, and I'm sure others could benefit by applying some of those too!"* My idea was simple –I wanted to help entrepreneurs and coaches attract more clients and make more sales without spending lots of money on ads, complicated funnels, or having a big following.

I know that as an entrepreneur myself, I certainly didn't want to spend thousands of dollars on advertising. I also didn't want to be bothered with anything complicated. I wanted something simple and straight forward so I could get results the fastest way possible.

I started to test out the market to see if this is something that other entrepreneurs wanted help with. I posted on Facebook with the message *"Would you love to attract 10 clients in 2 days? Comment 'YES'"*, and I got a lot of responses. This showed me that the market wants to be making money.

I continued to post on Facebook, did Facebook Lives, a 2 Day challenge, and ran a free training offer to test my idea. From those activities, I was able to book calls. I listened to the challenges and goals that the entrepreneurs and coaches had. I offered them my solution – the "Sale A Day System" which you can access here (https://www.asaleaday.com) and kept tweaking my offer until it was a perfect fit for the market.

The Sale A Day System keeps the focus on the number one thing in any business, <u>sales</u>. There are only three main things that matter for making consistent sales: Attract-Book-Convert (ABC). Using my experience, I've stripped out everything else and just focused on the key strategies to make sales. I kept it simple, effective, and also make it the fastest way possible for my clients to make money.

The market loves it! I quickly sold the Sale A Day System program multiple times, and I still do! I gave the market what it wants and, equally important, I was able to deliver results. My clients were making sales after sales after sales. It truly is a blessing.

The Reward

Since then, I continued to be of service to my niche – helping them with consistently attracting clients and making sales. I'm also pleased and thankful that I'm able to run my business from anywhere in the world.

I love to travel and am now able to treat my family to nice vacations around the world. Right now, I'm writing this book in Malaysia where my family and I are spending the summer together. I've been invited as an honorary speaker to three prestigious universities to talk about "technoprenuership" (technology and entrepreneurship. Yes, I've also been attracting, booking, and making sales while traveling!

I leased a Ferrari F488 for my husband's birthday, and he had the biggest smile on his face. He works really hard for the family but rarely treats himself. I'm so happy that I'm now in a position to make his dream come true.

I was interviewed at *Fox TV* as one of the female leaders discussing the challenges and solutions for entrepreneurs and coaches. I was personally invited to attend the "Make Your First Million Female Entrepreneur Retreat" in Bali, and that totally exploded my business.

My book, *She Made It Happen*, just hit the #1 International Bestselling List in multiple countries! What a blessing to be sharing my story and inspiring others to make things happen in their life and have the best possible future. Grab your copy of *She Made It Happen* for just $0.99 today at:

https://www.amazon.com/dp/B07X3NL14N

Equally as important is that I get to have fun and hang out with my family. I'm there for all their moments sharing the joy. I also get to spend some "me" time. I love to bake, watch movies, and read books. I'm so happy and thankful for all the blessings!

The Brightness of the Future

I'm now scaling my business to seven figures and beyond (anything is possible, right?). I continue to give the best service to my clients through my existing programs:

- **Make A Sale A Day System** – Attract more clients and make more sales without spending a penny on ads, complicated funnels. or having a big following;
- **6 Figure Savings System** – How to consistently save money and structure towards financial freedom;
- **Bestselling Online Program** – 7 Steps to create a successful and profitable online Program;

- **UpLevel Mastermind Program** – How to scale your business the fastest way possible;
- **Brand Power Publish Your Book** – Publish your own bestselling book to help establish your authority and gain credibility, and be featured in hundreds of global media to reach thousands of your ideal clients.

I'm working on several new programs for my clients to help them take the next step- the "6 Figure Trainer System," to help my clients make money through speaking gigs and corporate trainings and also venturing out into corporate training to help companies increase their sales and profits.

I'm really excited to be releasing two more books next year *Make a Sale a Day Without Ads, Complicated Funnels, or a Big Following* and *From Zero to Success – Inspiring Stories of Successful People Around the World.*

I look forward to chill out and explore the world with my family. What a blessing to be helping millions of amazing entrepreneurs, coaches, consultants, and business owners from around the world to make money and have the best possible lives!

The Wisdom

Knowing what I know now, the three things most important things that I can share with you that will help you to make money in business are these:

1. Make it about the market. Tweak your offer so that its exactly what the market wants;

2. Listen to the feedback and iterate your offer quickly until you get the magic formula – a perfect fit between you and the market;

3. Be consistent, persistent, and committed no matter what happens. These are the secret ingredients to your success.

"Stand in Your Power! You are WORTHY of success and money." – Izdihar Jamil

Success Actions

Here are three powerful actions that you can take right now to make things happen in your business:

1. Write down who your ideal clients are. For example, are they professionals, entrepreneurs, coaches, business owners, corporate clients, etc.?

2. Invest in yourself by purchasing suitable Program, Coaching, Seminars, and book in the next 30 days to help you grow and learn about business and making money.

3. Post on Facebook and/or other social media every day for 30 days and start attracting those ideal clients.

Love and blessings,

About the Author

Dr. Izdihar Jamil
Money Coach & Consultant, USA

Dr. Izdihar Jamil is a money coach and consultant who lives in California with her husband and children. She has a Ph.D. in Computer Science and uses her technological skills to accelerate her success.

She loves helping entrepreneurs, business owners and coaches to attract more clients and make more sales in their business so that they can have the best possible lives!

Her methods are proven, simple, and effective. They are designed to produce the fastest results possible for her clients.

She is also a bestselling author. Among her titles are *She Made It Happen* and *Make a Sale a Day Without Ads, Complicated Funnels, or a Big Following* (upcoming!). In her spare time, she loves reading and baking for her family.

Contacts

- **Business Name**: Diamond Queen LLC
- **Website:** https://www.asaleaday.com
- **Email:** izdihar@asaleaday.com
- **Facebook:**
  https://www.facebook.com/izdihar.jamil.1 , or
  search for "Izdihar Jamil"
- **Instagram:** @izdiharjamil
- **LinkedIn:** https://www.linkedin.com/in/izdihar-
  jamil-ph-d-97236598/ , or search for "Izdihar
  Jamil"
- **Current Products/Services:** A Sale A Day
  System, 6 Figure Savings System, Bestselling
  Online Program, UpLevel Mastermind Program,
  She Made It Happen (bestselling book), *Make A
  Sale A Day* (upcoming book) and *From Zero to
  Success* (upcoming book),.
- **Ideal Clients:** Entrepreneurs, Coaches,
  Consultants, and Business Owners.

- **Facebook Page for All Readers and Fans**:
  (Tips, Strategies, Ideas, Inspiring Stories to Make
  Money Fast In Business)
  **https://www.facebook.com/groups/makemoneyf
  astinbusiness/,** or search for "Make Money Fast
  in Business"

Relentless Focus

By Amanda Rush
Online Marketer, USA

"When you succeed, you party. When you fail, you ponder. All greatness comes from pondering." - Tony Robbins

The Ordinary World

From unemployed, in debt, and unable to find a job, to building her own six-figure online marketing business from scratch. This is the unfinished story of Amanda Rush.

The Drama

In early 2016, I was in college and struggling. Although my schooling was affected, the struggle was not due to school itself. It was due to lingering emotional challenges leftover from my troubled teenage life.

Instead of dealing with this emotional trauma, I turned to alcohol. I drank too much and too often. The biggest problem was when I drank, my negative emotions came out. It would be either uncontrollable rage or uncontrollable sorrow. Either way, my life was going downhill fast. I started mistreating my loved ones, almost lost the love of my life, and even dropped out of school.

The Turning Point

It was at this extremely low point that I stumbled upon an online course that promised to help me find "The Good Life." I bought it with what little money I had saved in the bank from my cashier job, and that's when everything started to shift.

I started reading books on the topics of health, wealth, love, and happiness. I started learning about a better way of living. I learned about entrepreneurship, and a spark was ignited.

The Vision

With my newfound wisdom, I knew I wanted to start my own business and build a life I previously didn't think possible. I dreamt of a day I could provide for my family, create a world of prosperity and freedom, all while doing work I actually cared about. I knew the sky was the limit.

Once I had this vision of what could be, I started searching for more courses. I wanted to learn from people who had already succeeded at what I wished to achieve. I bought course after course, mainly on the topic of online marketing. I learned a lot, but I still wasn't really getting anywhere. Then, in April 2016, I bought yet another course, but this one would change my life forever. This course taught me what it really takes to build a vastly profitable business from nothing.

The Call to Action

Now, this course teaches you how to build a business doing anything, but I chose to do marketing in the fitness industry.

Why?

For one, I'm an introvert, and I felt as though I finally found a career where I could spend hours and hours every day alone yet actually make a difference in the world. Second, I've always been a creative yet analytical person, and marketing seemed to be a perfect fit for these qualities. Third, I am passionate about fitness and knew this was an industry in which I'd love to be involved.

I felt as though I had really found my place. I had found an amazing dream to work toward. I worked relentlessly for hours every single day learning and building.

The Downfall

All was going well until I re-introduced alcohol into my life. Since my problem didn't seem to be an addiction but rather an emotional problem, I felt it was safe to drink again now that my life felt great. I was wrong...

After a while, my emotions started to take over once more. I became an angry, hostile drunk as my teenage trauma reared its ugly head and started taking control of my life again. I started to lose sight of my entrepreneurial dream. I started being a not-so-good person again, and I almost lost everything – again.

At this same time, I left my job as a cashier and started working as a sales consultant at a luxury vehicle dealership. This gave me the illusion that I was doing better in life, and I lost the drive to do something great with my life. I lost focus.

Then, things got even worse. I had gotten in trouble with the law due to my problems with alcohol, and at the same time I got fired from my job selling cars. With the legal proceedings taking hanging over my head, it was impossible to find another job. I was unemployed with bills to pay and even the most low-paying jobs that wouldn't hire me.

After hitting yet another rock bottom, I had had enough. I stopped drinking and decided to turn my life around for good. I still have never looked back. It was late 2017 when I truly decided to turn it all around, and the year to follow was one of the hardest years of my life. It was a year of struggling to get back on my feet and attempting to fix all of the mistakes I had made. I remember it like it was yesterday – my wife and I sitting on the floor, crying because we had no money and no way to make ends meet, and having to rack up debt our credit cards just to afford groceries.

Then, I finally caught a lucky break in December of 2018 and found a job delivering newspapers. It was seven days a week from 2 a.m. to 5 a.m. for only a few bucks a day. It sucked, but it helped pay the bills. That's when things finally started to take a turn for the better.

The Key Ingredients

Rewind just a little bit to the beginning of 2018. In the background, I had been using this time of struggle with no income as an opportunity to ponder my life once again. I was able to refocus on my dreams of which I had previously lost sight. Since I had no job to take up any of my time, I wanted to make the most of it. I worked eight to 12 hours a day on building the future I wanted. I even created a rigorous schedule of mental fitness training, hard work, and physical fitness training – and, actually stuck to it.

This went on for a whole year, and I had no results to show for it. Part of the problem was I had been side-tracked by my need for money. I started focusing on niches I didn't really care about, but ones that I knew I could make a substantial profit from such as the solar and heating, ventilation, and air-conditioning (HVAC) industries.

What I found out the hard way is that people can subconsciously tell when you don't truly care, and I didn't truly care about the industries I was targeting.

Now, fast-forward to December 2018 again when I got that newspaper delivery job. Now that a little bit of money was flowing in, I was able to think more clearly and refocused on my passion – fitness. I started reaching out to personal trainers and nutrition coaches. They could tell I was sincere, passionate about the industry, and that I truly cared. And finally, my business started to take off!

The Growth

In January 2019, I finally had a successfully running business. I was getting clients consistently, and my business was growing. I was beyond grateful; I was happy and excited!

A few months later, a business-mindset coach reached out to me. He asked me if my marketing system would work for his business. A lightbulb turned on in my head as I realized I'd be able to get him quality leads. So, we started working together on his campaign, and it was a success!

The best part was that I now had a system that I knew would get amazing results for not just fitness coaches but a much wider range of professional coaches and consultants! Due to this revelation, my business continued to grow at an ever-increasing rate.

The Reward

I am now running a successful business online. I'm doing something I love with complete independence, and I feel so grateful every day. I get to work from my home office in a beautiful house in a great neighborhood. My family and I can finally enjoy nice dinners out. We get to attend fun events and shows. And, we can finally travel which has always been a dream of ours!

The Brightness of the Future

I am now working on scaling my business even further. I'm also starting to become an authority figure in my field, which is such an honor! I am constantly looking for better ways to serve my clients, add value, and improve my services. In fact, I'm now building an online course to show coaches and consultants how they can consistently get more clients for their business. I know I am making a positive difference, and I can't wait to see what the future holds!

The Wisdom

Now that I've gone through some really tough times and come out the other end even stronger, I want to share some advice.

First, don't ever give up on your dreams. When life feels the hardest, that is your chance to create something great.

Second, always focus on your area of passion. You will know if you don't care about your niche, and so will your prospects. I mean it! Focus on that and block everything else out until you reach your dreams.

"It's pretty much impossible to be good at everything, but it is surprisingly easy to be the best at one thing." - Sam Ovens

Success Actions

1. Brainstorm your passion and where you could provide the most value;
2. Pick just one thing;
3. Focus on providing value in this area and don't waver.

To Your Success,

About the Author

Amanda Rush
Online Marketer, USA

Amanda Rush is the founder of Sphynx Media, an online marketing agency that helps coaches and consultants get clients. She is making a positive ripple effect on the industry by helping many coaches reach more people and helping them to create a greater impact on their clients' lives.

Amanda is an online business owner and fitness enthusiast. She lives with her wife and two dogs in California. Before she started her business, she spent seven long years at junior college studying psychology, art, math, physics, and engineering before finally finding her passion and creating Sphynx Media.

Contacts

- **Business Name:** Sphynx Media
- **Website:** http://sphynxmedia.com
- **Facebook**: facebook.com/amanda.rush.33
- **Instagram**: @_amandarush_
- **LinkedIn:** linkedin.com/in/sphynxmedia/
- **Product/Services**: The Perfect Client Generator
- **Ideal Clients**: Coaches & Consultants
- **Dedication**: To my wife, Kristen for unconditional love and support along this bumpy journey.

- **Facebook Page for All Readers and Fans:**
  (Tips, Strategies, Ideas, Inspiring Stories to Make Money Fast In Business)
  https://www.facebook.com/groups/makemoneyfastinbusiness/, or search for "Make Money Fast in Business"

Decisions: The Pathway To Power

By Azlin Ishak
Financial Educator, Malaysia

"It is in your moments of decision that your destiny is shaped" – Anthony Robbins

The Ordinary World

Azlin grew up in Malaysia in a middle-class family that was quite comfortable. She migrated to the United Kingdom at the age of 24 in the year of 2000 to pursue an extraordinary life and financial prosperity. Because she was entirely unprepared, life as an immigrant was very challenging. It had pushed her from being comfortable into a struggle to just to survive. The best job she could get at that time were being a cleaner, washing dishes at schools, and working in a printing factory. Her first paid job was £3.10 an hour. She felt very insecure by not having any family or friends in a foreign country, so, she thought that she had to work four jobs a day from 5 a.m. to 10 p.m., six days a week. She was regularly verbally abused and harassed. At the same time, she found out she was suffering a psychosexual problem called "vaginismus" and

43

struggling in her marriage. She was always lonely, scared, and depressed. Her self-esteem gradually deteriorated.

The Turning Point

After two years of struggle, her life got much better when she had enough money to pursue her Master's degree, got a better job, and her husband got a job. Unexpectedly and not long after that, she got divorced. She left her marriage and home with nothing. This put her in a position worse than before. She was now jobless, broke, homeless, and depressed. She couldn't see any light at the end of the tunnel. It was pitch black, and she was at the brink of giving up on her life.

One day she met an amazing lady who invited her to a self-development program. Through the program, she surrounded her herself with empowering people who supported her. Azlin learned that her life did not work because she did not take 100% responsibility. Her focus was on blaming herself, other people, and situations. She had enough of a life that was full of dramas and sadness. She made a decision that her life is going to work because she is going make it work – whatever it takes!

The Vision

The pain that Azlin went through when she was homeless had made her want to be a landlord providing affordable and comfortable houses for people. The pain she had to go through being broke drove her to manage her finances so she could help other families to plan and manage their finances well also. The hurt of suffering vaginismus had forced her to be brave and being a support for couples to help their marriages work.

She made a decision to make her life work and help others so they don't have to go through the pain she went through. Failure was not an option for her.

The Call to Action

The new decision she made has directed Azlin to a new cause, direction, and actions. She started to work seriously on her psychosexual problem, vaginismus, by getting professional help. She started to manage her finances religiously by implementing what she learned through financial literacy programs she attended. She decided to re-marry her ex-husband to give themselves a second chance. Even though she was broke, she decided to spend a lot of money on self-development, financial literacy, and property-investing programs.

One of the first things she did was raising her standards, thereby changing what she demanded of herself. She wrote down all the things she would no longer accept in her life, all the things she would no longer tolerate and the things she aspired to become.

The Downfall

Regardless of her efforts, the on-going challenges with her vaginismus persisted, she was still broke, her marriage was still an uphill struggle, and her life improved only just a little bit for the next two years. She wanted to be a landlord, but she kept failing to raise enough money to start investing in properties. She never missed any treatment sessions for vaginismus, but she did not make any progress. It was like hitting a brick wall. She felt frustrated and started to doubt herself.

Somehow, by making the new decision to make her life works <u>no matter what</u> gave her the power to keep on changing her approach despite her frustration and doubts.

The Key Ingredients

Azlin had determined that no matter what decision she made, she would be flexible, look at the consequences, learn from them, and then use those lessons to make better decisions in the future.

She practiced being fully aware of these three important decisions that she made in her life on a daily basis:

1. The decisions about what to focus on;
2. The decisions about what things mean to her;
3. The decisions about what to do to create the results she desired.

When she failed to raise enough money to start investing in the properties she wanted to invest in, she focused on the solutions to overcome that problem. She wrote down all the possible solutions and decided what and when to take actions in order for her to achieve her desired results. For her, the lack of money was not a problem, but it meant challenges and adventures in her endeavor.

As a result, she focused on looking for below-market-value properties until she found three of them. She also focused on finding investors who trusted her so they could raise the money together. Whenever she made a bad decision, she decided not to make a drama out of it but to learn and use the lessons to make better decisions in the future.

Azlin now is a landlord with a portfolio of properties in England and Malaysia that she rents out to families and students.

In her pursuit of overcoming vaginismus, she changed her approach many times until she finally adopted a holistic approach in healing herself, combining the distinctions she learned from the self-development programs she attended and sex therapy. After a few months, she had a breakthrough in overcoming vaginismus and never had the problem again in her life.

The Growth

Azlin decided to move back to Malaysia after 14 years in England. The pain she went through out from being uninformed and irresponsible in her financial life in the past has motivated her to help people to plan for financial life. She decided to start a new business in financial-planning consultancy. She sat for an exam and gained a license to be a *Takaful* (Insurance) Advisor in Malaysia. She started small as a *Takaful* Advisor, and now she has an agency called Al-Wakeel Advisory with 15 team members. Al-Wakeel Advisory has helped nearly 500 people in their financial planning.

Azlin started with RM180,000 ($45,000) revenue in the first year, and today the team is in progression towards half million Ringgit Malaysia ($125,000) of revenue. She is passionate about educating her community to be financially literate, able to take control of their financial life, able to manage their finances, and able to achieve financial independence. As an act of giving back, she runs a weekly, free, financial literacy class for her community.

Al-Wakeel Advisory has also helped women to create a career and passive income through their financial consultancy business while having the flexibility being a mother in raising their own children. The agency provides strong and reliable training system to the team members. It is crucial for the team members to be knowledgeable, committed, and trustworthy to protect the Malaysian community wealth.

The Reward

Just a few months after overcoming vaginismus, Azlin conceived a baby boy, and she treasures her motherhood. As she was earning passive income from her properties, and by managing the property portfolio from home, she was able to be a stay-at-home mother, enjoying her motherhood and raising her own child. It has been a privilege for her to be able to take care of her own child while still earning income for the family. For her, being a mother is the most important career in the world as she believes mothers shape human souls and help build the character of future generations. Now, she is a proud mother of two amazing and lively children.

Azlin currently employs a staff to look after her properties. Through her properties portfolio, Azlin enjoys passive income and has increased her net worth significantly.

She also has created a partnership with her husband in becoming committed and passionate parents in raising great children. As a result, their marriage has grown stronger and stronger.

Azlin also enjoys passive income through the team she created through her financial-planning consultancy business, Al-Wakeel Advisory. Through both these businesses, she has created passive income which gives her freedom to be involved with her growing children's activities, travel the world, and run free, financial-literacy classes for her community.

Her self-esteem and satisfaction sky-rocketed as she feels she is making a difference to her family, tenants, and community.

The Brightness of the Future

Azlin now is gearing her business towards RM1,000,000 ($250,000) revenue and expanding Al-Wakeel Advisory to 50 team members in 2021. She decided to start building a property portfolio in Malaysia and work on her mastery of investing in the Malaysian property market.

It is her dream to create a free, financial-literacy club helping 100 members achieve their financial goals. She gets indescribable satisfaction and pleasure by growing herself through her business and contributing to the community.

In the future, her dream is to help thousands of women overcoming vaginismus through her own products and services. She believes with help, guidance, and the right therapy, women can overcome vaginismus easily, freeing them to enjoy a fulfilling sex life and embrace their sensuality.

The Wisdom

Azlin learned to utilize the forces of pain and pleasure to create lasting changes and improvements she desired for herself and those she cared about. She experienced pain through suffering vaginismus and being broke and homeless that has caused her to hit her emotional threshold. Finally, she made the decision to use her personal power, take action, and change her life. This was the magical moment when pain became her friend.

Whenever she sees other people in pain, she also suffers. It hurts her to see people in financial mess, homeless, or suffering vaginismus. She discovered that when she took action and helped these people through their troubles, her pain disappeared. For her, pleasure means being able to provide affordable and comfortable homes for people. Pleasure means educating and helping her community to take control of their financial life. Pleasure means seeing other women overcame vaginismus and other marriage challenges. As a result, she has created businesses that she is truly passionate about and believes in.

By learning to use pain and pleasure to your advantage, you do not have to rely solely on your willpower. Willpower can run out. but the "big why" you have created through your pain and pleasure will help you take decisive actions towards your goals. Whenever you are feeling pain, do not numb yourself. Feel the pain and use it as a powerful force to move you towards your goals.

The power making decisions gives you is a tool you can use to harness your personal power. You can literally change your life and business the moment you make a new decision. You know that you have truly made a decision when actions flow from it. When you decide, you cut other possibilities and excuses. A lot of people do not decide and let others and circumstances decide for them. Not making a decision is a decision in itself, and that can be a very bad decision to make.

To strengthen your decision-making muscles, Azlin practices making decisions often. In the past, she could not even decide what she wanted to eat for dinner! In her decision-making practice, she made many bad decisions along the way, and she decided to learn from them. When she learned from the bad decisions, she makes corrections without invalidating herself or others.

You will learn to make good decisions by learning from bad ones. Keep on changing your approach and strategies until you achieve your desired goals.

"Life is either a daring adventure or nothing." – Helen Keller

Success Actions

1. Write down one action you need to make that you have been putting off and why you have not taken the action. Maybe you need to start taking control of your finance. Maybe you need to lose some weight. Try to decide if taking action is more painful than putting it off.

2. Be aware of the cost and the impacts if you do not make the change and take action now. Write them down. Imagine and feel the pain, cost, and impacts on you that will occur by putting off taking the actions. Intensify the feeling of the pains. Be aware of the pleasures you will gain by accomplishing the action. How do you feel – liberated, joyous, relieved? Make an extensive list that will drive you emotionally to take action.

3. Make a decision to take or not take the action.

For your success and freedom,

About the Author

Azlin Ishak
Agency Owner, Malaysia

Azlin is a mom of two energetic boys and married to a doctor. She is a successful agency owner, financial adviser and property investor. She is committed for people to have successful finances so that they can look after their family and future.

Contacts

- **Business Name**: Al-Wakeel Advisory
- **Website**: www.azlinishak.com
- **Email**: mailto:azlin.ishak@outlook.com
- **Facebook**: https://www.facebook.com/lin.ishak, or search for Azlin Ishak
- **Products/Services**: Investment Plans, Trust Funds, Managing Family Finances, Team Building, Coaching, and Consultancy
- **Ideal Clients**: Agency owners, professionals, families, business owners

- **Facebook Page for All Readers and Fans**: (Tips, Strategies, Ideas, Inspiring Stories to Make Money Fast In Business) https://www.facebook.com/groups/makemoneyfastinbusiness/, or search for "Make Money Fast in Business"

A.R.T: Attract, Retain, Transform

By Arooj Ashraf
Business Growth & Brand Strategist, USA

"Unshakeable purpose is often born from trauma. You can perish under pressure or rise and become the catalyst for transformation."
– Arooj Ashraf

The Ordinary World

My life has been anything but easy, but the hardships taught me to be more attuned to the needs of those around me. I was always the sensitive child; words landed harder than intended. Criticism sparked the need to overplease, and rejection was the final destination, never a detour. These are decisively some of the most terrible traits and beliefs any entrepreneur can have running in their subconscious mind, and for years, they crippled my success.

Later on in this chapter, I share how I reframed these beliefs to ignite my purpose and help other women scale multi-six to seven-figure businesses without overextending themselves in pursuit of their dream career and financial stability.

The Drama

As a survivor of numerous narcissistic encounters which left me financially crippled and emotionally and psychologically battered, I have made it my mission to help women become financially independent so they never have to stay in unhealthy situations. I help women become ICONS in their industry so they can attract their ideal clients, retain their loyalty, and transform lives without hustling, chasing, overdoing, and collapsing from burnout. This A.R.T. Method is one part of my signature program that has helped business women reshape their business into efficient cash-generating machines.

As women, I find we are our own toughest critics, holding ourselves to a higher standard. I urge you to remember that in order to become an ICON, you have to first affirm: "I CAN." That includes a balance of, "I can do anything I set my mind to, but honoring that just because I can does not mean I must do everything." Stop overcomplicating your business. Your ideal clients are interested in results, not a marathon of tactics that exhaust them before they reach the finish line.

My clients have managed to reinvent their careers from barely surviving to blissfully thriving in under nine weeks using customized strategies that leverage their unique strengths, or as I like to call them, their "Superpowers."

I was not always a business strategist; in fact my zone of genius was always telling stories. I did not become an intentional entrepreneur until the demand for my creative work meant "Uncle Sam" required his share. So, I set up a humble LLC as a branding agency serving small businesses and nonprofits offering a one-stop-shop for all their marketing needs. In offering everything, I designed the agency to self-implode because everything depended on my time and creativity. I made all the mistakes I see novice entrepreneurs make, and in telling my story, I hope you will be able to bypass these common hazards and build a business that is profitable from day one.

In the past decade, I have built five businesses; some did very well while others struggled. With experience, I have discovered every successful business that scales predictably has three distinct elements: a unique solution differentiating its position in the market for a validated problem, a memorable story, and consumer-centric values that are reflected in the service, delivery, and mission of the company. In other words, there has to be a viable demand for a solution that your business provides. The message has to resonate with the client's needs, and the service, quality, and delivery have to supersede expectations, especially for a premium product or service.

The Turning Point

My first venture into entrepreneurship was actually a complete accident. I had no intention of actually selling my art. However, my creativity was always the easiest way for me to make money. While other children were selling lemonade, I was selling paintings, paper-mâché decorations, handmade jewelry, crocheted tops, and ceramic sculptures. My greatest struggle was that I could never predict what someone would love and pay for. So, I created what I wanted, and most of that work is still displayed around my family home.

I did not realize it then, but I was operating from a fear of rejection. When something did not work out the way I hoped, I did not insist on figuring out the missing piece. Instead, I let my creative brain wander off to shiner objects. I firmly held the starving artist's belief and never envisioned becoming a career artist. Instead, I became a journalist (a step slightly above being a starving artist) to a financially malnourished professional.

As a strategist, I love designing solutions with the least possible resistance to achieving massive goals. That is exactly how I completed my undergraduate degree in two years with numerous internships, a vast portfolio of leadership awards and accolades to boast about. As a journalist, I mastered two critical skills: how to ask pointed questions to get to the core issues for absolute clarity, and how to explain that information in the simplest form so anyone can understand it. I adopted the concept of KISS: "Keep It Simple, Stupid." And with KISS, I discovered the shortest and fastest way to achieve a goal was to reduce resistance in its path. I had not, however, mastered this skill into business practice, and the lesson showed up in my life as heaps of resistance.

The Downfall

Any time I excelled and overachieved, sabotage would set in, and I would lose everything. My first job out of college was an absolute nightmare. I was graduating early with high honors and two possible dream jobs. I lost them both in the same week due to circumstances beyond my control. In my devastation, I chose to work with a tiny, ethnic newspaper whose owner had a very large personality and an inflated ego to match.

Spotting a multi-talented, hard-worker, the owner exploited my talent and energy every way possible. From extending my workload to that of four people to requiring I work longer than 12-hour days to complete deadlines she created out of thin air. She would often demand I return to the office after midnight and threw hysterical fits if I refused to pick up her phone calls in the middle of the night and listen to her dramatic stories of men she claimed were obsessed with her.

At one point, I was working for less than $2 an hour, and she would find reasons to dock my pay. Sounds illegal, right? It was, but with a bruised ego riddled with self-doubt and no idea how to set professional boundaries, I stayed stuck much longer than I should have. This was my first difficult encounter with a narcissistic vampire and sadly not my last.

The pattern: Lessons not learned and mastered repeat.

I stayed in horrible situations because the voice inside my head told me I could not do it alone. This voice also came from other people, like my parents and former mentors who were all dealing with their own lack-of-worth stories. Of the many lessons I can share from this experience, I would like to highlight three; know your value, set your standards for self-respect high, and get comfortable saying "No" when your boundaries are tested.

But what does this have to do with making money fast in your business? Everything... Your ability to receive money is instinctively linked with your self-worth.

I hated money. I associated people with money as exploiters, mean, evil; and since my perception of myself was that of a kind, loving person, I created a belief that I had to struggle to make money and could never keep it. In fact, any time my bank account hit above $10,000, self-sabotage would kick in – unexpected expenses would arise, and life would crumble back to "Struggling 101." It never seemed to matter how much I saved or how well I budgeted and tracked my finances.

While all the businesses I started were profitable from day one, I struggled constantly to scale. The only way I knew how to earn more money caused me to be overwhelmed, sleep-deprived, and ultimately burn out completely. The key to my initial success was very simple: I was showing up authentically, building real relationships, and sharing my passion and creativity. Unwittingly, I was branding myself as an expert because I spoke with confidence, commitment, clarity, and produced results. These 3Cs in combination with measurable results is the essence of infusing cash into any business. I was filling a demand, a gap, before creating an intentional product and service. This 3Cs+R formula is what I use to access the potential for profitability for any service business I consult with.

The greatest setback to my career and life showed up in the disguise of love. The kind of love that felt divine, like a soulmate connection. We all know hindsight is 20/20, and what I thought was the perfect man showing up like an answered prayer was actually a covert narcissist ready to exploit and take. Together, we created magic. With my talent and ambition at the helm we built an award-winning photography business. To satisfy my creative itch, I built a thriving cultural art business. To keep his insatiable appetite for stealing money from me at bay, I helped him design a passion business based on his skills. From the outside, we had it all: genuine friendship, thriving businesses, and a gorgeous home. The reality was that I was exhausted from the constant mental abuse, defeated from the financial exploitation, and drained from the emotional turmoil that comes from living with a narcissist. I describe my as life as with a live leech slowly draining the essence of life from my heart.

I have never been a quitter, and sometimes when you don't bend for life, it breaks you. This time, staying in a soul-sucking situation was not just a financial jeopardy, it was literally costing me my life. When things are not working or unnecessarily difficult, take a step back and observe where the problem is. This time the problem was me trusting a partner who was unfaithful not just in marriage, but also in business. I had a choice. I could continue to suffer and be exploited yet again or dissolve two thriving businesses, abandon my dream home, and move 1,500 miles to start over from scratch.

The Vision

Heartbroken, betrayed, and broke, my self-worth could not have been any lower, but I mustered up my strength and left. I was fed up with building my dreams only to lose everything. Something had to change, and the only person I had control over was me. I turned to my natural talents to sustain me, and as a brand photographer, I encountered a phenomenon that irked me. The businesswomen with multi-six figure businesses kept telling me I was lucky that I had the choice and financial means to leave my marriage and start over.

The Call to Action

Frustrated and furious, I began investigating why I was hearing this message from women I perceived as well off. I realized many of them were one bad month or breakdown away from losing everything too. They lived in constant fear scenarios of "what if...," because their businesses were not structurally sound. They were so focused on presenting their successful image that they failed to address how to generate the funds to sustain their business. The natural gap-finder and fixer in me stepped up, and as I laid out how they could make more money without losing their minds, I realized my life's struggle and lessons were actually an apprenticeship on what not to do in business. I was determined to help change their business approach, but first I had to change my own story and self-sabotage patterns.

This turning point led me to create my consulting program with a strategy framework I call the "Triple Amplifier," or "TriAmp Method." Every time a client applied these strategies their business, it became easier to manage. Their profits tripled overnight, the floodgates opened, and clients came pouring in. One of my favorite clients, Jody, a retired nurse practitioner, was able to earn $35,000 from one in-person presentation selling the services we created based on her passion. I will layout the simple formula she applied to earn money with ease.

I applied the same three critical shifts and matched my previous annual income in the first month of launching my consulting business. Here are my three essentials to creating a profitable business from day one.

The Key Ingredients

I.   Prosperity Mindset

Frown and groan all you want. My financial situation did not progress until I debugged my hidden sabotaging beliefs that were formed as an infant. My perception for mindset work is deeper than just analyzing thoughts, journaling, and/or meditating. For me. mindset work means uprooting the behavior patterns and habits that lead to failure and show up in various ways for my struggling clients.

Reprograming your mind goes deeper than reciting mantras 24/7. It demands the courage to look at your darkest beliefs objectively, trace back their origins, then make a commitment to replace these beliefs through sustainable actions. Ask yourself the tough questions that make you uncomfortable. Evaluate your relationship with money – what it feels like having it, receiving it, giving it, and asking for it. Then create a new story and relationship with money, integrating this story in your life consistently for 90 days.

Recognize that mindset work is an ongoing process – the deeper you dive, the more there is to uproot. Find tools that help you refocus and align your relationship with money exactly the way you want to receive, spend, and grow it, then commit to using these tools daily. For my clients, I offer access to many processes and experts that I personally tried and had success with. However, this is a very personal experience, and what worked for me may never work for you. Trust that reshaping your money story will unlock financial success faster than any strategy I can create for you.

II.   A Product that Sells Itself

The most common mistake I see entrepreneurs make is creating a product and then trying to build demand for it. To create a business that is profitable, focus on getting results you can deliver even if you were hanging upside down from a bridge. Well, maybe that is a bit too dramatic. However, if you show me a problem, I can instantly show you the gaps and chart a map to the solution. I do this constantly while stuck in traffic, grocery shopping, and traveling. It is the easiest thing for me to do. It is my Superpower, so I charge premium for it.

Are people always asking you for help with a specific problem? If you can create a simple framework or system that leads people from their unique frustration to their desired outcome, you have a viable product that can sell itself. However, if no one is interested or confused by the offer, the cost to produce and deliver significantly outweighs what people will pay for it. In that case, you need to spend more time in the brainstorming phase. No amount of fancy marketing, clever social media promotions, and graphics will sell a product no one is looking for. If you do not have any ideas for the business, reach out to the people around you and start looking for patterns in the problems they are experiencing in their lives.

Your business is not very likely to be reinventing the wheel. Most businesses are based on inspiration from others and serving a pre-existing need that clients have. The question to ask is not what you are doing for your clients, but how are you doing it better than anyone else in the market.

Where are the gaps in the industry that no one else is fixing? I believe the most ingenious solutions are so simple they are obvious, but everyone wants to be the next great innovator, so they overlook the basics. Remember the 3C+R formula: confidence, commitment, and clarity. My client, Jody, a retired nurse, used this simple formula to generate $35,000 in sales from one presentation. She had a simple desire – to help young nurses avoid adrenal fatigue and burnout so they can have a better quality of life and serve their patients. Her confidence index and ability to deliver the results was an 8 out of 10 because she related to their experiences. Her commitment to exceeding and delivering a unique service was a solid 10 because she knew it was an unmet need. What she was missing was the clarity of HOW to create this program in a way that got them results without overburdening them.

III.   Undeniable Leverage

To stand out in a crowded market, you need to be able to differentiate your business from the rest. Your clients need a clear and concise message that sticks in their head like a Christmas jingle that tells them the exact results they can expect. Creating a brand story and precision positioning it in the market means your competitors will become irrelevant to your ideal client. For Jody, her brand positioning was simple: she knew exactly what her ideal clients were experiencing. Her ability to articulate their pain in their language and show them a simple map outlining how she was able to avoid all the pitfalls made Jody an expert they instantly admired. Jody was giving them exclusive access to something they desperately wanted, and she made it easy to participate.

The Reward

Now, there are certain flaws and limitations to Jody's business that are by design. She wanted to keep her business as simple and concise as possible, and she is not looking to scale to seven figures. Jody's mission thrives on personal interaction and individual transformation. She has created a truly heart-centered business that is creating meaningful impact in the lives of her clients who will then improve the lives of everyone they come in contact with.

Jody's business is a contagion of hope, and that is the secret ingredient to unmatched prosperity.

> *"Success for me is testing ideas, failing, and revising until you find the right combination of elements that produce predictable results."*
> – Arooj Ashraf

Success Actions

Here are three simple action plans I suggest you implement to convert your business into a profit-generating machine.

1. **Unshakeable Focus**: Determine what you are exceptional at and create a simple, replicable process that can be implemented easily to achieve the desired results. Focus on one product/service, one clear, concise message, one outcome, and one market. Establish yourself in this market as an expert and over-deliver on your promise of results. If you have done the required research and crafted framework based on data, you will only need to make minor adjustments to your processes.

2. **Mutually Profitable Partnerships**:
   Businesses that are built-in silos fail much faster. Be very strategic in identifying partners who serve the same clients, have the same standards of excellence and align with your business mission and values. Build a relationship where your clients get better results because they are benefiting from both services.

3. **Feedback Loop**: Your work is never done. There is always room for improvement, and the best way to serve clients is to create a feedback loop where you always know three things about your clients.

   a. What were they experiencing before they sought out your services?

b. What solutions did they try before yours?

c. Why did they wait to seek a solution?

d. What were their expectations before?

e. What was their opinion during the process or after the results?

f. What is something they wish your program included?

Having an effective feedback loop will create an experience bank for all your marketing. The patterns that will emerge will not only help improve your signature program but will also lead to further product or service development.

I believe every woman has the ability to create a million-dollar empire from her heart-centered passion, and my mission is to help her create it in the most efficient way possible.

Money is the tool that will help you transform lives for the better and create a lasting legacy for your family, and I hope to join you on this journey of unlimited success.

Yours in ambition,

About the Author

Arooj Ashraf
Business Growth & Brand Strategist, USA

Arooj Ashraf is a serial entrepreneur with 15 years of experience working with multi-million dollar organizations and non-profits. She has owned several multi-six figure creative businesses as a photographer, graphic designer, and writer. Her passion is building profitable businesses with heart-centered women who are on a mission to transform lives with their work. Arooj's Superpower is helping women recognize their true talents and leverage them into profitable, passion-based business that scale rapidly. She loves working with precision rather than gimmicks and is a rapid problem-solver committed to getting to the root of the problem and correcting it effectively.

She grew up on three continents and loves traveling near and far, exploring cultures, exotic landscapes, and connecting with people of the world. Most importantly, she is devoted to testing out all the possible desserts she can. By creating her consulting empire, she hopes to build a coalition of millionaire women who join together to make this world a better place for future generations, one transformation and life at a time.

Contacts

- **Business Name**: Arooj Ashraf Consulting
- **Website**: www.aroojashraf.com
- **Email**: info@aroojashraf.com
- **Facebook**: https://www.facebook.com/TriAmpMethod/?ref=bookmarks or search for TriAmpMethod
- **LinkedIn**: https://www.linkedin.com/in/aroojashrafmba/ or search for Arooj Ashraf
- **Products/Services**: TriAmp Method: 9week Business Acceleration: Zero - 6figures, Cash Infusion Strategy: 90 Minute Strategy Creation, Million In One: Full Service Business Incubator: Scaling to $100K Month
- **Ideal Clients**: Heart-focused businesswomen with established businesses ready to scale rapidly to 10X their joy, wealth, and influence and become ICONs in their industry

- **Facebook Page for All Readers and Fans**: (Tips, Strategies, Ideas, Inspiring Stories to Make Money Fast In Business) https://www.facebook.com/groups/makemoneyfastinbusiness/, or search for "Make Money Fast in Business"

The Will to Win

By Dr. Hanim Romainoor
By Dr. Hanim Romainoor
Graphics Consultant and Lecturer, Malaysia

"Many of life's failures are people who did not realize how close they were to success when they gave up." – Thomas Edison

The Comfortable World

I am going to share my story about how a successful businessman shaped my will to win. It is someone who is very close to my heart, someone I love and respect dearly. He is a resilient man, a responsible brother, and a loving family man. He is my dad. He has the vision to win new projects and new business. I am sharing this story so that the world can know his strength, will, and success.

To tell you the truth, I was not born to be successful in business. Instead, I was born into a comfortable life built by my dad, a hardworking man. My full name is Nurul Hanim, but you can call me Hanim. I was born in Kuala Lumpur, Malaysia. I was raised in a humble town in Selangor, Malaysia called Hulu Langat. I have two brothers and two sisters. One of my sisters has Down syndrome. I am, on the other hand, is the opposite of my dad. I really do not know how to be resilient. When I was younger, all I see from him is that he goes to work comes back home late and makes sure everyone sits together during dinner. My dad was also very strict. He makes sure I to do all the house chores. From sweeping to mopping to cleaning the windows, and to washing the dishes and drying the dishes making sure the dishes are placed back in the cabinet. These are the thing I hated doing. I prefer the maid to do all the house chores.

The Ungrateful One

My life was very comfortable. I grew up in a five-bedroom house with each room having its own toilet. Dad hired a maid to do the house chores for us. To be honest, I was pampered. I got all the fancy toys, branded clothes, expensive shoes, and enjoyed luxurious vacations. It turned out, I was a late bloomer. I didn't know how to read until I was 12 years old. In the 3rd grade, my teacher asked me to read in front of the class, but I couldn't do it, so she tried to force me demanding, *"Stand up and read!"*

I stood up, and I couldn't even spell out the letters. I didn't know how. I was confused with letter B and the letter D. I cried in front of the class and felt ashamed. But, it was not my dad that gave me moral support. He was not that kind of mushy person, but he did have my mother help me through my education and learning process. She is a smart and educated woman.

My mom inspired me to be an independent woman. *"To be independent, you need an education,"* my mom said. I know, I was not doing so well in high school, and I thought I wouldn't be able to be like my mom, a smart and educated woman. But my mom believed in me. She saw that I loved drawing and I learned faster interacting with computers than from books. So, she enrolled me into a multi-media school in Serdang, Malaysia where I was able to learn computer graphic design, computer languages, and media technology. There, I learned to be an independent adult learner. I worked hard to earn my diploma until I got to go to New Zealand to do my college degree and finally achieved a high distinction. My dream to be independent was achieved. I started working and job-hopping around several private companies for a total of four years. Later, my mom made sure I earned my Master's and Ph.D. degree, which I completed in Perth, Australia.

You see, I was a pampered child, and I grew up to be a pampered adult. I did not understand resilient. My success was all from my mother's support. I am thankful to have had her as my mother. However, I did not learn the will to win. My dad was always strict with me, but he never thought me how to be resilient – or so I thought.

Healing from Emotional Suffering

I love learning in New Zealand and Australia. I fell in love with Perth. I had the luxury of being free, experiencing a new culture, having the adventure of my life with lots of late-night laughter and no chores. I was then living in Penang, Malaysia and working in Universiti Sains Malaysia as a Senior Lecturer in School of The Arts. Some may have said my life then was complete. I had a Ph.D. degree. I was married to a supportive man. I'd completed paying off my first car loan, and I bought my own house. But I was not satisfied with my life.

I hated being a lecturer. I felt trapped in a world where I had to teach routinely because my adventurous life was taken away from me. I was just like the commentator in a football game, one that was never a player. I was always complaining, judging, and comparing my life to others around me. I was not happy.

I remember my dad yelled at me saying, *"You don't need an education! You only need to stay at home and become the maid."* His words broke my heart. I could not stop my tears. From then on, I swore to him I will be the wealthiest person in this house with the highest education and a successful business. My parents were always the source of my aspiration. Their love was unconditional. I appreciated the scolding; it was his way to teach me to buck up and be responsible. Life is not all about finding the prince charming, flowers, and roses.

Becoming the Magnet for Business

I went through a lot of heartbreaks, took on a lot of responsibilities, and had a lot of failures. I've carried many burdens throughout my years. I never understood how to share them with others. I tended to hide them. There is something about heartbreak. It really does define whom you trust.

As for me, when my dad died, I didn't cry. That was not because I didn't love him. It was because I was all cried out. I couldn't complain. I was living in the dark, deep inside the whale's belly. I didn't trust even my husband with my loneliness. The thing about heartbreak is it either can break you or make you. When love was taken away from me unexpectedly, it shaped me.

"What do you want? What do you want? What do you want?" I could hear my dad yelling as if he was next to me.

I yelled back, *"I want to forgive. I want to be brave. I want to love. I want to be authentic. I want to contribute valuable knowledge, experiences, reflection, and education to the community. I want society to feel I am valued. I want unity, compassionate, and loving fellowship,"* and I creep into the corner by myself crying, missing him.

I finally genuinely let go of the burden I have been carrying in my heart. I said goodbye to failure, goodbye betrayal, goodbye to lies, goodbye to regret, goodbye, anger, goodbye sadness, and I said bye-bye to the guilt. I stopped blaming others for my emotional pain. I ended my being the complaining cow.

Being Focused / Realization

Love comes in many different forms. It was hard to recognize when it was taken away from me unwillingly. I had to close my eyes, wipe my tears, and begin to see with my heart. I had to let go of attachment to feel again. I had to forgive my past for the sake of my future. I was done playing small and hiding my credibility because I didn't know how to trust. I decided that I cannot live a life as a complaining cow.

You know what? My dad did teach me how to be resilient. He taught me how to be strict, to be bold. Through his experience, he showed me never to quit when failure decided to drop by. He didn't stop; he just moved on to look for something new. That is how he attracted money into his business. I realized blaming others is the quickest way to give up my power, my will to win. That is why I will never be that housemaid, but I will clean the house as a maid does.

Remember, when I said, *"I will become the wealthiest person in this house with the highest education and successful business"?* Well, I was on my way to becoming just that. After I had detoxed all the burdens inside me, I became open to success. I became a magnet for new projects and new business. This is the will power that was waiting to burn from inside my heart, and this is the intangible lesson my dad wanted me to learn.

Comfort Zone, Self-sabotage

I quit! I am scared of judgment, rejection, and failure. The minute someone gave me a critique, I took it as negative feedback. The adrenaline rushed through my veins, and I felt my heart racing, sweat came out from my skin, and the burden came back all because I was so scared of these three things: judgment, rejection, and failure. I was my own worse judge. I was too strict on myself in everything I did. I was not open to new opportunities.

I found myself overwhelmed with good intentions – a lot of things to do, a lot of things to give, and a lot of old baggage to let go. My life became chaos. I kept falling and stumbling, never finishing the task I had started out to do. I was face-to-face with becoming a resilient woman. I was hustling but kept falling, again and again, never winning. My world became disorganized. My head was confused; my car was dirty;

my house was cluttered; my office was cluttered; everything was in a mess. The easiest way out was to quit.

I began self-sabotaging what I want by always retreating back to my comfort zone. Being outrageously open to success was uncomfortable. I am not used to having people authentically attracted to me. To trust people and give them my trust was an arduous task to do. I didn't trust myself to let go of this heartbreak. I had no closure. I began to creep back into my comfort zone. The feeling of loss, betrayal, and anger was familiar. I went back to feeling lonely. I missed the love I had, the love I'd lost. I was angry at the betrayal people seemed to throw at me. I continued to distrust and buried my feelings deep inside, keeping the familiar feeling of grief and sadness. I lost my dad.

The Key Ingredients

I needed a change of attitude and Practice! Practice! Practice! Practice! Of course, my dad passed away, but his legacy stays. His successful business did was not started from sitting around complaining. His successful business came from his attitude, his attitude to be resilient, to win. I often get scared of questions such as what you want to have. Most of the time, my answer would be, *"I don't know what I want."*

Now, though, I know what I want. There is a 50/50 chance of getting what I want, but it will never come from quitting. When I stop trying, it means I will fail 100% of the time. Hearing my dad's screaming, scolding me, telling me to be a maid, gave me the courage to take the risk to be open and trust people because <u>I will</u> prove him wrong. I am authentic, brave, and valuable. I have the will to win. I have an iron will!

Growing Strong Roots

I admit, to change my being from having negative energy to positive energy was really hard. It took a lot of will power to want to win. If I hadn't wanted to win, I might have become the maid my dad wanted me to be today. If I hadn't wanted to win , I would probably just be staying at home not knowing how to read. It took a lot of guts to confess that I was a complaining cow. I stopped blaming myself. My growth process was messy. Family, friends, and colleagues noticed my change in attitude. They asked, *"You look more cheerful and bright lately. What is your secret?"*

Despite being genuine and authentic to myself, I still feel I can easily be influenced by others, especially their negative energy. To change my energy and embrace growth took me a lot of courage to let go of old habits. It took a lot of commitment to be authentic. It took a lot of bravery to trust people. And, if everything falls apart again, I know now it will take a lot of forgiveness from me to let go and love again. If it happens again, I know now how to keep grounded because I have the will to win. I am not too timid to speak my mind.

The Reward

I am now the head of the Department of Graphic Communication in a prestigious university in Malaysia. I am proud of having a Ph.D. in Philosophy in Design. I am pleased to have mastered the artistic and communication skills required in Graphic Design. I am grateful for my talent in Computer Graphic Design, which is a bonus and an excellent tool for business and marketing and sales. I am currently working on a book cover and layout project.

My new being is pure. I am now authentic and can be a contribution to the other person. I will continue to grow stronger. As a metaphor, *"Grow a firm root and become a stronger tree. Avoid being the kite that is quickly being pushed around by the wind."*

Despite being ambitious in my job, balancing work and family life is essential. After 11 years of marriage, I am now a mother of two beautiful children. I gave 100% trust to my husband, and I appreciate his support all these years. I enjoy spending more quality time with my family. I want more family quality time to see my children grow.

You know what? I had the will-to-win all along. My dad taught me that intangible lesson long ago. I just never realized – it was a lesson.

The Will to Win: The Magnet for New Opportunities

This change led me to opportunities that have been knocking at my doorsteps, asking for collaboration. I also hold a position as a graphic consultant to a startup company called Simple Century Sdn. Bh.

Many family and friends reach out to me, and I know that my new positive vibration is attracting them. My will to win attracts and open doors to new opportunities, new networks, bigger networks, and trusting connections.

I am contributing my time to make new leaders. When I do a masterclass design, it is as if I am the coach in a football game. I engage with the class, and when the students learn a skill and feel appreciated, I know I have done my job in creating successful students around the globe.

I am looking forward to sharing more fruitful masterclass workshops and to passionately write and share my reflections. I want to make my dad, the successful businessman proud, and to tell him, *"I proved you wrong."*

Let's say I like teaching now. It is exciting meeting new people from different backgrounds. I don't look at it as a repetitive routine. I see it as a unique opportunity for me to create new connections to collaboration.

I am scaling my visibility to include more wide networks, and I am ready to play big and to win big. My dad's energy runs inside my veins. It is the power of my intention to gain new lead.

The Wisdom

The will to win did not lead me to play the hard call to win. I am already a winner. I have always enjoyed continued blessing from my mother, my husband and family, and friends. I am genuinely open to others while being authentic with myself. I trust myself that I can achieve when I focus and put my mind onto whatever I want to make. And when I do, I know I will achieve it.

Reach out to people that need support. Let everything happen. Be at peace with yourself with no obligations to the bank, people, animal or material things.

Contribute to helping others. You will never know when the light that you have given will become the path for someone else to escape difficulty. When you are allowed to help others, take it because you are answering someone's else's prayers. Nobody is using you. Remember, you are the magnet for business.

"You are being presented with a choice: evolve or remain. If you choose to remain unchanged, you will be presented with the same challenges, the same routine, the same storm, the same situation, until you learn from them, until you choose change. If you choose to evolve, you will connect with the strength within you, you will explore what lies outside the comfort zone, you will awaken to love, you will become, you will be. You have everything you need. Choose to evolve. Choose love." – Creig Crippen

Success Actions

Here are three success actions that you can take right now to make things happen in your business:

1. Be open;
2. Be authentic;
3. Get up and try again.

Warm regards,

About the Author

**Dr. Hanim Romainoor Graphics Consultant &
Lecturer, Malaysia**

I am a Senior Lecturer in Universiti Sains Malaysia,
Pulau Pinang in School of The Arts. I am also a graphics
consultant.

Contacts

- **Business Name**: Hanim Romainoor
- **Website:** https://scholar.google.com/citations?user=O2zrOR8AAAAJ&hl=en
- **Email:** hanim.romainoor@gmail.com
- **Facebook: - Hanim Romainoor**
- **Instagram: hanim_romainoor**
- **LinkedIn:** https://www.linkedin.com/in/hanim-romainoor-486599120/
- **My Products/Services: Graphics Consultancy**

- **Facebook Page for All Readers and Fans:** (Tips, Strategies, Ideas, Inspiring Stories to Make Money Fast In Business) https://www.facebook.com/groups/makemoneyfastinbusiness/, or search for "Make Money Fast in Business"

Wake Up and Be Clear!

By Ija Juhari
Interior Designer cum Financial and *Takaful* Adviser, Malaysia

"Debt is great source of inner unhappiness."
– Debasish Mridha

The Ordinary World

I, Ija Juhari am a single mother to my beloved son, the Future Captain Eesa Putra. I worked as an interior designer for 18 years, and now I am a fulltime wealth adviser and also passionate about my dream to travel around the world by train.

The Drama

When I came back for good to Malaysia, I carried a small amount of savings. I thought that the money would help me survive for few years. But, I totally forgot about the reality of life. The cost of living in Kuala Lumpur is high, and I met new friends and was enjoying my life like there was no tomorrow. I also started joining with a few friends to invest in businesses and other money schemes.

After a few months, I checked my bank account and was tremendously shocked to find that I had lost most of my savings. Nothing could be done. All the staff and everything else needed to be paid. I was furious and started using my credit cards and maxing them out. I had to do this with all seven of my credit cards and take out a personal loan just to cover all my obligations.

I thought it would then all be over, but one day I finally realized I was in debt for several hundred thousand Malaysian ringgits (US$50,000).

At that point, all of my so-called "friends" walked out of my life and left me alone. From that moment, I knew that I had made a huge mistake to trust people with my money.

The Turning Point

The debt I had was making my life so miserable that in 2016, I took drastic action. I went to every bank to get my balance statements. I combined and calculated all debts, and it became my worst nightmare. I cried looking at the amount and asked myself repeatably,
"How am I going to settle all this debt?"

My total debt was nearly a quarter million RM (US$63,000)!
Shocked? Yes! But I have faced my fears – the fears of the truth. The truth that I was afraid of how much debt I had. I know you might be afraid of how much debt you have but ignoring the problem will never make it go away.

No one ever wants to be in debt, but for sure, everyone had to stop living in denial. Telling myself, *"My debts wasn't that bad"* or *"Others are worse"* or *"Just pay a minimum, as long as you pay"* just didn't help me.

My turning point was the debt amount and my age. If I wanted to buy a house before I was 40, I needed to settle this debt as soon as possible.

Throughout all the years, I carried this debt around with me. I needed a reality check and to stare down exactly how much debt I had and what it would take to get out of debt. The first thing I did was to be certain of how much my debt was. How much would I need to pay every month, and how long would I need to pay until I could clear it all?

Secondly, I had to figure out why I was in debt and stop doing those things again. I cut up all my credit cards. I cut down on all unnecessary subscriptions. Basically, I had to tone down my lifestyle – by a lot.

I wrote down every detail of the debt on a piece of paper, and I stuck it on my wall. Every day I looked at it and asked myself, *"How am I going to settle this debt?"* When I saw it every day, it really killed me, and it forced me to work harder.

Finally, I had to find a way to earn enough money to repay the debt. To save money looks so easy when we have a high salary. But, it seems impossible when your monthly payments on your debts alone are 90% of your salary. And that does not include all the necessities!

This was my turning point and led me to discover how I could make my first six-figures in savings in one year and successfully buy my first and second houses within that same year.

The Vision

I would like to help people to get out of debt and start saving more for their future and to have better protection and create passive income from a variety of sources.

To settle almost quarter-million RM of debt within three years is not impossible because I've done it. You just need to know who knows how and talk to them.

The secret is to find the right solution, and it's free right here! Don't ever trust money scams, multi-level marketing (MLM), or any services that require you to pay big, upfront fees. You don't need money to make money.

But you need money to pay your debts.

The Call To Action

One day I discovered a program. It is actually a government program to develop a personalized debt repayment schedule. I went there, and they provided me with a program – and it's free!

What a relief! I was feeling lighter again.

This program actually lengthens your payment period for another 10 years, so your monthly commitment is reduced. With this program, I reduced my monthly debt commitments by about 40% .

Even though I managed to reduce my monthly payments, I was not really enjoying the fact that my debts would only be settled after 10 years, and I would be 46 years old before I could buy a house. I was sure a house by then would be super-expensive, and the mortgage payments would be higher.

So, in that case, by hook or by crook, I must finish all my debts off before I'm 40, in just four years' time.

The Downfall

So after the pact, here comes another problem. One of my biggest problems was my salary was not enough for me to achieve my target. If I want to settle the debts within four years, I needed to pay at least fifty thousand RM (US$12,500) per year. That is nearly 75% of my annual income. It was still not sufficient for me to save more and live comfortably.

I was frustrated because I was so content with my life with just working as a fulltime interior designer. Business was really not an option after I was trapped in this debt for few years because of my lack of business knowledge. I know not everybody has to earn more money to get out of debt, but it sure makes it a lot easier.

The Key Ingredients

I had to take the risk. That was the only answer. I had to face my fears and do whatever it takes to meet the challenges. Living with debt and paying the minimum amount every month wouldn't help me to save money, plus I would end up paying more than what I now owe.

In 2016, I started working a part-time job and running an online business. I pledged not to invest in anything above RM100 (US$25). Without a big cashflow, I had to find something that was a low-risk business. I sought knowledge from books, people, forums, and also few websites.

Finally, I found a way to settle all my debts – the "Snowball Effect":

    1.   Target small debt:

2. Pay double the monthly amount;
3. After settling the smaller debts, take all the money from those monthly commitments, and;
4. Start doing the same for some of the larger debts.

You will find this method works. If you don't have enough money, you need to find an extra income

Create new income, both passive and active income. Passive income will give you more time and help to create your financial freedom.

The key in this program is to be disciplined and focused.

The Growth

I am sure everyone values their life differently. But we all must have something in common. To be happy and wealthy is something everyone wants in their life. How can we change our lives and be better? Getting out of debt and starting to save money is something you can start today.

The Reward

I found my dream house! Finally! Yeaaa!

My biggest motivation was to be out debt so as not to carry them around until I die, and so I could buy a house. It was my dream to own a nice house with big yard sitting in front of a park to watch my son when he was playing in the playground.

I find the most rewarding thing is spending my time with my family, especially with my son. I used to be someone who was so busy with work! I worked until late at night. Sometimes, I had to leave my son for few days, weeks, or even sometimes for few months.

The result was that it turned out my son didn't even think of me when I was away. He is okay when I'm not around, but he thinks of his granny all the time.

There was a time he cried and had a fever because he missed his granny after just a few days living with me. That really hurt my feelings.

But now, I have all the time I want with him. It's the best feeling ever as a mom.

The Brightness of the Future

I am now pursuing my fourth passive income in online business doing furniture consultation. I am currently working on *Hibah Takaful* for an Islamic protection plan website and also do Islamic wealth management for heritage and heirs.

I am planning to take few exams on investment, and maybe that will be fifth passive income endeavor. I am writing my life's journey *Berbaloikah?*, and I hope it will help women to be a better wife and better mom.

I plan to do more volunteering work in and outside Malaysia and join many spiritual retreats while traveling all over the world.

The Wisdom

Have faith in yourself when nobody else does. That is the most important thing in your life, and you can stop self-sabotaging your success. Self-sabotage involves behaviors or thoughts that keep you from what you desire most in life. Actually, your desire is making you grow. If you have no desire, your life will be dull.

Tony Robbins says the strongest human need is growth. *"If you are not growing, you're dying."*

Sure enough, the more growth you experienced, the more confidence you've gained. The more you give, the more you will get. If you want love, give it the best you can. If you want to grow your business, help those around you grow theirs. If you want certain connections and contacts, share yours with others.

Practicing the law of giving is actually very simple. In fact, the easiest way to get what you want is to help others get what they want. This principle works equally well for individuals, corporations, societies, and nations. If you want to be blessed with all the good things in life, learn to silently bless everyone with all the good things in life

> *"Happiness depends on your mindset and attitude."* – Roy T. Bennett, <u>*The Light in the Heart*</u>

Success Actions

Here are three success action that you can take right now to make things happen in your business.

1. Get it all down on paper.
2. Make it measurable.
3. Build a success mindset.

All the best,

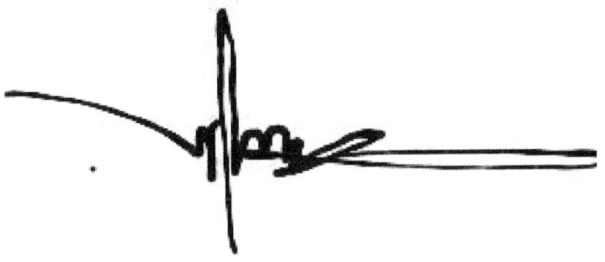

About the Author

Ija Juhari
**Interior Designer cum Financial and *Takaful*
Adviser, Malaysia**

Ija Juhari lives in Seremban with her son and is also very experienced interior designer who has experience working abroad in the UK, Middle East, and Malaysia.

She is a single mother, and she's rocking it!

She is passionate about design and also designing her own method of saving and clearing off hundreds of thousand RM of her debts within two and half years.

She is a very happy-go-lucky person. She loves to write and inspire people through her writing on Facebook.

She also loves cooking.

Contacts

- **Business Name**: Misi Bebas Hutang
- **Website**: https://www.misibebashutang.com/
- **Email**: ijajuhari_mbh@gmail.com
- **Facebook**: https://www.facebook.com/madina saliza or Search for "Ija Juhari"
- **Instagram**: @Saljuzari
- **LinkedIn**: https://my.linkedin.com/in/saliza-juhari-72967a82
- **Current Product and Services**:
    - Misi Bebas Hutang, Hibah Takaful (website),
    - *Berbaloikah?* (upcoming book)
- **Ideal Clients:** Entrepreneurs, Young Couples, Professionals and Business owners

- **Facebook Page for All Readers and Fans:** (Tips, Strategics, Ideas, Inspiring Stories to Make Money Fast In Business) https://www.facebook.com/groups/makemoneyfastinbusiness/, or search for "Make Money Fast in Business"

Decision and Faith

By Nikoleta Djordjevic

Success Happiness Coach, NLP Trainer, Serbia

"A journey of a 1000 miles begins with a single step." – Lao Tzu

The Ordinary World

I grew up in a small eastern European country named Serbia. Although the outside circumstances were not in my favor, especially when you were born in a "bad economy" and in the middle of a war, I decided to take a chance in seeing and experiencing the world outside of my geographical boundaries. I lived in China for about two years, and now I am living in Croatia, pursuing my dreams and enjoying every moment that life has to offer. My two favorite things are dancing and traveling. Both of them fill me with enormous gratitude and respect toward people from all around the world knowing that we are more same than different.

The Drama

Back in 2016, two key things happened almost at the same time that marked my future/ My now-ex-boyfriend and I broke up after more than five years of a relationship, and I was fired from a company where I extremely loved to work. My life until that moment was perfect. I had a job that I loved, my finances were more than great, and the people who I used to work with were absolutely gorgeous, determined to succeed, productive and open to learn and grow. I led a team of five as an operations manager, and I was supposed to move to America. I had a wonderful relationship with a man who really appreciated me for who I am, and we really thought we were going to spend the rest of our lives together. A dream come true, right? Great job, great relationship, what else do you need in life?

First my relationship fell apart, and not long after, it was my job.

Although in my mind, I was already in America pursuing my American dream being a successful and happy businesswoman, things didn't work out well. It was a hot July evening in 2016 when I received a call and was fired. In shock, I just hung up and went for a walk thinking of how my life would look like from now on. Everything I planned turned into dust.

Having a personality like mine – proactive, in motion, constantly seeking options – helped me to move fast from that situation. I didn't think a lot about what I was going to do next. Actually, I quickly made a decision on my next step, and I didn't think about anything else except for this: I decided to take a break for the next two to three months, take a backpacking trip around Europe, and then move to China. Most of the people would ask me, *"Why China?"*

My answer was simple, *"It was the furthest place where I could be just with myself and process what had happened over the last couple of months."*

One side of me was super excited. I love traveling, I love to be in an international environment, and I know I am capable of adapting to any situation that I put myself in, like a chameleon that changes its colors so as not to be caught by a predator.

The other side of me was terrified and wondered, *"What the heck am I doing?"* China? No job, no friends, nor anybody who I know who can be of help? I didn't know how I was going do that. I didn't feel super confident. Actually, it was completely the opposite. I thought nobody would love me again, and I thought I was not worthy of having a decent job.

I couldn't tell anyone that I was more scared than I looked from the outside. I played the super-confident young woman that knows what she is doing, and at the same time on the inside, I felt ashamed, lonely, weak, and wondered why this happened to me. I was a victim in my own eyes. However, the decision I made was firm, and I jumped into the unknown with faith that everything would be all right without knowing exactly how.

I found a job as an English teacher very quickly after I landed in Shanghai. That was all I needed. Working as an educator in a relaxed environment was a "Bingo!" at this stage of my life. Work was perfect, and as much as I didn't have any trouble doing an amazing job, it was not as easy socially as I thought it would be at the beginning.

All the logic that worked in Europe didn't work in China. Cultural differences, language barriers, the environment, social life – everything was so different. Culture shock hit me before I realized it. I had ups and downs every month for the first six months. One day, you would see me extremely happy, amazed by all the differences between the European and Asian culture, and the next day I would swear at every single difference and wonder what in the name of the God I was doing there. These negative feelings hit me especially during the holidays and on a birthday when I missed my family and friends. The first three months there were just crying, working, and trying to deal with everything by myself. That was a time in my life when I didn't want to share my feelings with friends because I felt sorry for myself, and I couldn't let them see me weak.

The Turning Point

When Serbian people leave Serbia, their decision is permanent. They go to look for a better future in the next country, probably stay there forever and never come back. From the very first day I knew this was not my permanent decision. I knew I was not going to stay in China forever, and that this was just a temporary solution until I figured out where and what to do next. Still, I knew my soul was seeking to express itself in a different way. I knew I was born to create a life that would help inspire people to take control of their life. When the roller coaster of emotions stopped, I could clearly think of what I wanted to do with my life.

I knew I liked the freedom to decide what I wanted to do and where I wanted to work. I knew that I wanted to decide when I was going to work and when I was going to have vacation. Since a very young age, I had this little voice that guided me in the direction of owning something that is yours, but I had never had the courage to actually step out of my comfort zone and start creating it. I didn't know if this was the right decision, but I had to try. At least, my Myers Briggs Personality test says I am a born leader, and if we are realistic, there are not really a lot of positions where you have the freedom to be as creative as you want, to build your own services, and to work with people that you want to work with. The only solution was becoming an entrepreneur. So, in the summer of 2017, I decided I was going to become one.

I bought a program that teaches people how to start their own online business, and very quickly I started with my first recruiting company. I want to be clear that I had no idea what I was doing, and I believe many of us who start a business have no idea how most of the things work. We just have a vision, make a plan how to get to that vision, give all that we have to succeed, have faith it will work, and adjust along the way if it doesn't.

The turning point for me was when I finally realized that recruiting was not my true calling, but I was a step closer. I helped many people get jobs and change their circumstances but still didn't feel like I was doing really something important and meaningful for them. I wanted to help people to truly get life-changing experiences, to realize that anything is possible if they only set their minds to feel happy. My destiny is to help people transform their life from the inside out. This is where the true potential sits and waits to be awakened. I did this and still do it with myself, and I help people do the same. At the end of 2018, I was getting into the life-coaching and training business, and my life got a completely new direction.

The Vision

I always believed you can have everything in your life: great career, loving relationship, superior health, and lots of money. I realized this belief is my superpower. No matter what situation you are in now, no matter how bad or good it is, it can always be better. The only thing you need is a decision. Making a decision is a mental move which will solve enormous problems for you in a millisecond. It has the power to instantly change any personal or business situation you will ever encounter. Almost every successful person says you should bring decisions fast and change them very slowly, if ever. The second ingredient of success is faith. Once you make a decision on what you want, you don't have to know how will you get there. You just need faith that you will figure it out.

Most of the people look at their current situation and make decisions regarding that situation. If they want to travel the world, they look at their bank account and say, *"I will travel the world when I make more money."* If they want to start a business, they say, *"I will start a business when I make enough money."* If they don't have a partner and still live with their parents, they will say, *"I will move out when I find a partner."* And what if I tell you that more than 95% of people think this way, and they are not happy with the results they get in life?

You have to make space for what you want <u>right now</u>. You can't desire something new and still remain where you are. You don't start a business when you have enough money. You start a business because you want it and you have <u>faith</u> in yourself that you will find a way to make it work. What happens then? When you are clear on your <u>decision</u> about what is it that you want and you have <u>faith</u> that you will figure out how to get it, your mental activity rushes in to find solutions, and suddenly you see resources all around.

I remember when I needed to invest a certain amount of money in a business mentor. At the beginning of my entrepreneurship, I barely could fund my monthly expenses, but I knew I would find the money because I made a decision that I wanted to grow my business and I had faith I was going to find it. And guess what? I did. Was it easy? No. But it was necessary for my success. I asked 20 people for help, and most of them said no. If we are absolutely honest, you don't need everyone to say yes. You just need one person that believes in you to reach for the stars. This is how decision and faith work powerfully together. I knew at this moment everything is possible and I promised myself that practicing to stick with the decisions I made until my objectives are reached will be one of my life goals.

The Call To Action

I've been spending day after day learning how to help people live happier, healthier and wealthier. I found out that people:

1. Do have personal and business goals but they have a problem moving from their current situation to their desired situation.
2. People don't have business problems; they have personal problems.

Here I found my skills and gifts useful. I am best at making people feel comfortable around me. I was honing my listening skills for years, and in my coaching business, this skill pays off. If you know how to listen, you can save your clients from suffering.

I work with people on raising their emotional vibrations and teach them how to become happy and aligned with their personal and business goals. I started very quickly practicing the emotional alignment with who they are and their mindset of who they want to become. We have to have in mind that not only our thinking changes our results, but we must take care of our emotions as well. I figured out that involving both, mind and emotions, gives profound results.

The Downfall

At the beginning, I wasn't sure that I had what it takes to help my clients get the desired results. I doubted myself, and I doubted everything I did. When I would speak with prospective clients on the phone, I would think, *"Who am I to do what I do, and why would anybody choose me over other more experienced coaches?"*, so I would just skip closing the deal. Luckily, when you know how the mind works, you get over these thoughts with lot of practice and repetition. This business is not about me; it's about my clients and how to help them live happier lives.

The Key Ingredients

People want to get unstuck and feel happy. No matter their personal issues or business issues, people want to be happy, and I knew I could help them live happier through my coaching services.

Decision and faith are two key ingredients that helped me keep myself on track, and I'm teaching them within my coaching service. Setting goals is never a problem, but having a clear vision and being able to tell it to another person that will understand what you want and developing the faith that what you desire will become a reality one day is what requires a bit of work.

The Growth

My focus is on helping people to overcome the inner barriers that are stopping them from achieving results, live in the present moment, nurture positive emotions, and achieve their relationship and business goals. I like to call myself a "Happiness Coach."

If you remember my story from China, it wasn't easy emotionally to set a balance. Through the inner work I did for myself, I could bring myself back and start my life as a confident, happy, and outgoing person. Since then, my emotions don't control me. I control them, and my joy and happiness level is at 8 on a 10-scale most of time.

My clients say that after only one session they feel lighter. After the whole program, I notice they are happier, no past hanging on their back and no negative emotions. Of course, life is not expected to feel happy all the time, but now they have control over their emotions, and they can decide how to respond to the situations and not react. Amazing people with amazing results who wanted to get rid of their past baggage.

The Reward

My reward is traveling the world, living in different countries, enjoying cat-sitting, and dancing kizomba!

The Brightness of the Future

I am developing a profound program that will transform people's relationships, business, and lives forever, growing businesses to six figures and making a new generation of prosperous and happy individuals.

The Wisdom

Always go for what your heart is telling you. Don't be afraid to try over and over and over until you succeed. Be decisive, and just start doing something. You will find a way how.

"It's not who you are that holds you back, it's who you think you are not." – Denis Waitley

Always be sincere with yourself. When you want something, say it. When you don't want something, say it as well. You are only one decision away from the life that you always desired. That's all you need. If you need help, it's okay to ask for it. We are not born alone, and we were meant to help each other.

Success Actions

Here are three success actions that you can take right now to make things happen in your business:

1. Write down what it is that you want;
2. Build a picture in your head of what type of person you have to become to reach what you want. Write all the possible details, what you see, what you do, how you talk, where you live, how does that person feel, etc.;
3. Read what you wrote every morning right when you get out of bed and in the evening before you go to sleep and see what happens!

About the Author

Nikoleta Djordjevic
Success Happiness Coach, NLP Trainer, Serbia

Nikoleta Djordjevic graduated psychology at the University of Nis Serbia. After finishing her studies, she worked in an American marketing company helping build the business and developing a language software. Love toward personal development and education was present throughout all her childhood and young age as she knew how important it was to invest in your skills which helped her to confidently move to Shanghai, China and travel the world by herself. She believes our mind is our biggest asset and we need to take control of it to make a life that we truly love living. As a typical millennial, she used to switch jobs often but that didn't stop her to pursue her own dream of becoming an entrepreneur. Eventually, all of the experience merged in one and now she's doing life coaching and development trainings for groups and companies. At the moment of writing this, she lives in Zagreb, Croatia and this is just the beginning of her dream life. Looking forward to the bright future.

Contacts

- **Business Name**: Loving Life Design
- **Website**:
  https://lovinglifedesign.wixsite.com/nikoleta
- **Email**: mailto:nikoleta@lovinglifedesign.com
  Facebook:
  https://www.facebook.com/nikoletatrainer
  Instagram:
  https://www.instagram.com/sagittarius_empowers/
- **Linkedin**:
  https://www.linkedin.com/in/nikoleta-djordjevic/
- **Services**: Mindset and Emotional Coaching, Development Training
- **Ideal Clients**: I help busy professionals and online entrepreneurs to bring their heart and mind together to achieve goals, let go of their past so they can live the moment, be happy and deepen the connection with other people.

- **Facebook Page for All Readers and Fans:** (Tips, Strategies, Ideas, Inspiring Stories to Make Money Fast In Business) https://www.facebook.com/groups/makemoneyfastinbusiness/, or search for "Make Money Fast in Business"

Authentic Alignment

By Dr. Sawiah Jusoh
Traveling Entrepreneurial Medical Doctor
UK, Malaysia, and Hong Kong

"The traveler walks through many mirages
before he finds water" –Yasmin Mogahed

The Ordinary World

I am a traveling doctor, a coach, and an entrepreneur. This is my story.

I grew up in a small town in Malaysia, and we were the most ordinary family you could imagine. My mother was a midwife for over 30 years, and my dad a hardworking civil servant. The youngest of three siblings, I was expected to work hard at school and strive for good results and a career, but nothing out of the ordinary. Everything was unfolding in the most normal and natural way possible until the day my father collapsed and died of a brain hemorrhage. Nobody was expecting this to happen. I was fifteen.

The Drama

Obviously, this day is imprinted vividly upon my memory because of the shocking nature of my father's death. It's also the day that my destiny was revealed to me, although I had no idea at the time. The best way I can describe it is it's as if I found the end of a thread that day, and I didn't know what it was connected to until many years later. You can call this fate or destiny if you like. Some people say that it's God calling you, and others firmly believe that you make your own destiny. I'm a doctor, so I'm a practical person, but what I can tell you is that something fell into place on a very deep level that day, and I didn't even know what to do with it, until many years later.

My father's death was totally unexpected, and I was at boarding school at the time. They sent me home immediately to be with my family.

I had never been on an airplane before as these were for rich people, and we were far from wealthy. My uncle paid for me to fly home, and by chance, the only seat available was in business class. I sat in the huge, luxurious seat that was far too big for me in the strange peace of a luxury cabin in the blue skies. The other passengers were business people with their heads full of meetings and figures, not schoolgirls sick with worry. Normally, I would have been wildly excited, but I knew that something terrible was unfolding. I could sense that this beautiful aircraft cabin, where everything was so enveloping and comforting, was cushioning me from the painful reality I would have to face when I set foot on the ground again.

I didn't want to cry or cause a fuss on the airplane. I kept praying that everything would be fine. I just wanted to be home. Even though my mind was filled with worries, I was conscious of the luxury of the cabin and the great hospitality on-board. The weight of the world was on my shoulders, and yet somehow, I was hovering above it, suspended in time as well as in the sky. I resolved that I would get through whatever came next, be strong for my family, and promised myself that I would fly business class again.

The Turning Point

My dad had collapsed unexpectedly and had been on life support for many hours by the time I landed. My mum made the decision to switch it off and bring him home to die a dignified and loving death surrounded by the family.

I arrived before my dad and saw him being brought home by the blue-lighted ambulance, his face covered by his oxygen mask. As I sat with him, I realized that I would never get the chance to speak to him again. So much had to be left unsaid forever, and yet it's hard to find the most basic words when you're faced with the final hours of life.

The Vision

I thought of my mum and sisters, and I made my second solemn promise of the day. I promised my Dad that I would become a doctor and make him incredibly proud of me. Although it was hard to put into words, it was as if my Dad could live on somehow through me if I achieved dreams and goals for him, rather than for myself.

My dad passed away shortly after this. I had a month off school to be with my mum, but I still had to study for and pass a big exam. My two sisters were both away, so it was just me and Mum for a while. She was grieving, in shock, and eventually depressed about my dad's sudden passing. I worked very hard to catch up with my missing work, and my teachers showered me with love and care.

The Call to Action

Fast forward many years, and I was a general practitioner (GP) in the United Kingdom. I was living a comfortable life on my doctor's wages. I was an employee and not very entrepreneurial, but I was contented and enjoying life. If I wanted something, I bought it. I settled my bills easily and was able to take care of my mother. However, life was about to push me far from my comfort zone to see exactly what I was capable of.

The Downfall

It was 2008. I was about to become a partner in a GP surgery when the economy began to collapse, and the partners pulled out. Overnight, I was unemployed with no money coming in at all. I couldn't afford my mortgage and was in danger of losing my house and car. I stopped opening letters and bills after a while and felt totally humiliated.

One thing I have learned in life is that wherever there is hardship, there are helpers – good people, with kindness to spare. My family and friends supported me, although I was embarrassed to accept their help, having been so self-reliant all of my life. I thought of my 15-year-old self, taking a cab by herself from the airport after her first flight, resolving to be strong for her family no matter how bad things were, and what she would think of my situation right now. I felt like a failure.

When a crisis hit, it exposed my weak points. My Achilles heel was my relationship with money. I was great at earning money, even better at spending it, but financially illiterate. I hadn't saved, and I hadn't taken out insurance or invested in anything I could liquidate to release funds, so there was nothing financially there for me at all. I was in a lot of debt. It took just one blow to knock me back down to the bottom of the pile again.

I was so humiliated by this situation that I became depressed. I even considered leaving the country, changing my name – anything to avoid the stress and humiliation of being a formerly high-achieving person that was currently unemployed. I pared back my lifestyle, canceled all of my subscriptions, and gave up all luxuries, but nothing seemed to help. I had never felt so hopeless.

As a doctor, I have to say that depression is a serious problem, and all of the symptoms I was experiencing were terrifying. It's important to seek help and be kind and compassionate to one's self when depressed. Looking back, I realized that these terrible feelings are not a punishment for a perceived failure, although it very much felt like that at the time. The times when everything feels so hopeless, extremely small and insignificant, are always the beginning of the most important turning points in life. I remember one of my mentors said, *"Human beings only emerge in emergency."*

The Key Ingredients

If I show you how I re-aligned with my core beliefs and priorities and kept an important promise to myself at a time in my life when everything was unraveling, perhaps it will help you to do the same in your own life. This can change your fortunes a whole 180 degrees overnight, and it can bring you riches, luxury, opportunities, and every possibility you can think of. More importantly, it allows you to grow as a person in the most authentic and joyful way. Looking back on my life and how it unfolded, I know that I would choose joyful growth and authenticity over money every single time, but there is no reason in the world why your life can't be full of all of these good things, or why they can't happen incredibly quickly.

There is a saying, *"When the pupil is ready, the teacher appears."* I was so very ready to learn my financial lesson at this point that somebody did indeed appear to show me the way. A friend took me under his wing, coached me, led me to the missing gaps in my knowledge and understanding of the world, and supported me. Among the many bits of invaluable advice my friend gave me was how to do cash flow. This was the missing piece of the jigsaw puzzle for me. This was the knowledge, understanding, and skill I needed, in order to truly fulfill my dreams. I realized I'd only been part-way up a mountain and tumbled down to the bottom. He was showing me how to get to the very top.

When my friend asked me what I wanted, I said I wanted to get out of this scary web of financial crisis. I wanted to have peace of mind and freedom in life. He firmly told me that it was not an easy path. I had to be serious about my why! I had to go100% full tilt with undivided commitment. It's true, the bigger the *why*, the easier the *how*.

That was the day I promised myself that poverty is not an option!

While everyone's journey is personal, there are some things that are universally helpful. I believe everyone should be financially literate, and it's never too late to start. Without this key, I would still be floundering now. If I can impart one other piece of advice to you through this chapter, it would be to educate yourself about money and never stop doing so.

The Growth

To cut a very long story short, I set up my own company and began to get some contracts. I had no income and nothing to lose. Growth was minimal at first, but I had an unusual way of doing things.

You see, when I commit to something, I strive for big results. I add values. I make a difference. I serve. It's just in my nature to do so. It brings me satisfaction and joy, and in this case, it brought me more contracts.

Over-delivering is a great strategy for marketing. By over-delivering, I get to "wow" my client and make them truly glad and grateful that they picked me for the contract. By over-delivering in a joyful way, I am not telling, but actually showing my client that it's me, my team, and them. We are on their side, and we have their back, which is such a precious and rare thing to find in the business world.

When I over-deliver, I no longer in competition with anyone else. Just like when I fly premium classes,

I am floating above the clouds. I am a part of everything, but at the same time comfortable and detached and able to think more clearly. I think part of the appeal of flying first or business class is that it feels a little similar to being "in the zone" – the state of mind where flow is effortless, and nothing feels heavy or difficult. By over-delivering, I was only ever in competition with myself because my usual competition was still sitting in standard class.

I began to build up my reputation and liaise with locum *(someone (physician or clergyman) who substitutes temporarily for another member of the same profession)* agencies. I recruited and referred other doctors to do locum work. I worked in partnership with a few agents to support me in this. My number one agent now is a managing director of an established locum agency in the United Kingdom.

When I connect with people, be it in business or personal life, the number one quality I looked for is a strong sense of responsibility and integrity, as I knew that this would guide them through any situation. My network and staff rewarded me over and over again with their hard work and professionalism, and they also began to succeed in their careers.

Having to live very frugally when I was unemployed, and even when I first got back on my feet, changed the way I looked at money. I realized that it was simply energy, and I needed to clear and refine my own energy first before I could realize my ambitions. I had to go back and re-align my beliefs, drive, and energy to one of the times in my life where I was incredibly focused, fearless, and determined, and didn't even realize it at the time. If you can find your own moment of realization, and I believe we all have them, it's almost like finding the end of a rope that guides you through a maze.

From then on, I had breakthroughs in my relationship with money.

Instead of buying more stuff, I began to feel grateful that I could pay for my mortgage and car, thankful that I could pay my own bills and not have to ask for help, and happy that I could invest in myself and my staff. This was "living the dream" to me, but the best was yet to come.

My company landed contracts with other healthcare organizations in the UK. In my career as a medical practitioner, I experienced working all around the UK and the world. In the UK, I had the experience of working in a private diet clinic where over 90% of the clients had a weight reduction of at least three sizes down. I supported the opening of many walk-in centers around the UK, working in three family planning and sexual-health clinics along the M4 – namely Cardiff, Bath, and Swindon. I ran a travel clinic in the busy London Victoria Station and ran medicals for CEOs and MDs of established companies in the UK through Nuffield Hospitals. I worked as an in-house doctor for a renowned law firm at Canary Wharf. I also fly the world being a civilian doctor to British Army and NATO (North Atlantic Treaty Organisation) bases.

The Reward

Today, I can have a full English breakfast in London, a stopover for light lunch, croissant, pastries, and latte in Paris, and a home-cooked dinner complete with Malaysian delicacies in Kuala Lumpur with mum and my family. On-board, I travel in premium classes in the first or business cabin. The world is my oyster. Most people live in one country at a time. Some live between two, but I live in three: UK, Malaysia, and Hong Kong. However, my real home is in the air, above the clouds.

My strategy for making money in business fast is not a trick. It's not an extra layer on top of the things that I would normally do to be successful in life. It's seamlessly built into the very fabric of everything I do and everything I want to achieve, and this is what allows me to live my dreams.

My chapter might be a little different from the other entrepreneurs in this book, as I am no longer striving to achieve the dizzy heights of my imagination. That is an exciting stage of life to be at, and you have it all ahead of you now – but I have already done it. Today, I have freedom around time, people, and places. I choose what I want to do, who I want to be with, and where I want to go. I can flip through a magazine and see a luxury resort, call the agent, negotiate the best deal, purchase a premium class airfare, choose my travel buddies – and off we go. Once upon a time, it was just a dream.

I did not only own businesses in the UK, but also a training company in Malaysia. I had a special interest in family planning and sexual health. I coached. My niche is psychosexual coaching. My coaching had no boundaries of place. I coached people from all walks of life and clients all around the world. I helped domestic-violence victims to get out of toxic relationships. I mediated good divorces, coached clients with vaginismus to have breakthroughs and cures and have natural conception and babies. Out of that, I have been blessed with a few godsons and goddaughters.

Now I live in three different countries and two continents: the East and the West.

Have you ever wondered what it's like to fulfill all of your dreams to the point to where you don't have to try anymore, and you can simply enjoy it all unfolding? Well, at that point, I guess you become a little like me! Maybe more relaxed, not so hurried and rushed all the time, but able to stop and smell the roses, to feel the rain, and to pay closer attention to the most important people and things in your life.

The Brightness of the Future

Being asked to write this chapter for the book has coincided with my return to coaching. I'm at the stage of the journey where coaching to me is the natural outcome of having followed the best advice and inspiration to its natural conclusion and found my own way of getting to my goals. While I'm selective about the clients I take on, I feel it's important to carry on the cycle of knowledge, wisdom, and guidance, having received so much of it myself. The process of empowering others is just as vital as empowering the self – the two things are linked in countless ways.

The Wisdom

I believe that the best investment in life is to educate one's self. With the guidance and support I had at the time, I attended many self-development and transformational programs. I invested in myself. I went to learn from world-renowned financial gurus, namely

Bob Proctor, Tony Robbins, Blair Singer, and Robert Kiyosaki.

Everyone's path in life is going to take them through good times and tough times. I believe we all have the seeds of greatness in us; we just need to nurture them. If you are facing a brick wall, a hard road, or a mountain in your path, look within for the answers. Think of when you were fearless and determined in the face of great hardship, and you will find one-half of the answers there. Think also of what inspired you and set your soul on fire, and there you'll find the other half. Combine the two, and your path will open up as if it's always been there, just waiting for you. Get support. Invest in yourself. Learn from the masters.

> *"A journey starts with a single step. You can travel the world over to find success and happiness. Yet if you don't carry it within you, you will never find one"* – Dr Sawiah Jusoh

Thank you for reading my chapter, and I hope that I have inspired you in some way to reach for your own destiny. May we all find our unique paths in life and become as inspiring as those who have inspired us!

Keep adding values and make a difference. Continue being of service.

Love and Light,

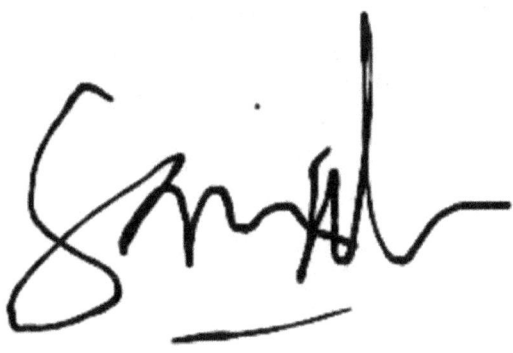

Sawiah

Success Actions

Here are three success actions that you can take right now to make things happen in your business:

1. Be financially literate. Do your cash flow. Know your numbers. Invest in yourself. Educate. Learn from the masters. Have a coach or mentor.

2. If you want to grow quickly, create a team and over-deliver. Go the extra mile, give more, outshine the competition by impressing your existing clients. There is no better marketing than an extremely impressed client.

3. Set goals. Put a structure in place. Get support. Honor the promises. Always add values and serve. Give your best shot in all your business deals.

About Author

Dr. Sawiah Jusoh
Traveling Entrepreneurial Medical Doctor
UK, Malaysia, and Hong Kong

Professionally, Dr. Sawiah Jusoh is a medical doctor with a special interest in family planning and sexual health. Being trained in the United Kingdom, at present, she considers being a doctor her passion rather than her job. She is passionate in her field and is committed for people to have freedom in their sex life, relationships, and sexuality. Born and brought up in Malaysia with Eastern culture and living in the UK for nearly a quarter of a century, she is dynamic in her approach, blending Eastern and Western culture. She has empowered men and women to have breakthroughs in this delicate area of sex and sexuality through psychosexual coaching.

Dr. Sawiah Jusoh is also an entrepreneur. She is the Executive Director of Wealth and Well Being Ltd United Kingdom. She was previously the Managing

Director of Success Precession Wellbeing Ltd UK and Success Precession Potential Sdn Bhd Malaysia.

A resident of two continents, Europe and Asia, and three countries, UK, Malaysia, and Hong Kong, she travels worldwide to inspire and make a difference in people to achieve their peak performance in wealth, health, well being, teams, relationships, and life.

A versatile, high-impact, in-demand speaker and trainer, Dr. Sawiah Jusoh has the unique ability to shake up the status quo and get people to change behavior and achieve unprecedented results. She has been invited as a guest speaker to appear at Konvensyen Jutawan Muslim (Muslim Millionaire Convention) 2012, was featured in online TV *ePower Women*, and on *Hello on Two* because of her great success.

Outside work and business, she enjoys learning from world-renowned gurus such as Warren Buffet, Sir Richard Branson, Jack Ma, Joel Roberts, Robert Pante, and many more. She also enjoys traveling with family and loved ones.

Contacts

- **Business Name:** Wealth & Well Being Ltd
- **Website:** http://www.drsawiahjusoh.com
- **Email:** coaching@drsawiahjusoh.com
- **Facebook:**
  https://www.facebook.com/sawiahjusoh
- **Instagram:**
  https://www.instagram.com/sawiahjusoh
- **LinkedIn:**
  https://my.linkedin.com/in/sawiah-jusoh-67579126
- **Products/Services:** Coaching – Psychosexual, Life, Success, Financial Literacy, Wealth
- **Ideal Clients:**
  - Men and women, who wish to have breakthroughs in life, success, wealth, cash, and/or sexual health;
  - Couples and singles who have issues in relationships;
  - Those with marital problems;
  - Women who suffered from vaginismus;
  - Domestic-violence and abused victims;
  - Ex convicts.

- **Facebook Page for All Readers and Fans:**
  (Tips, Strategies, Ideas, Inspiring Stories to Make Money Fast In Business)
  https://www.facebook.com/groups/makemoneyfastinbusiness/, or search for "Make Money Fast in Business"

Networking – Your Network is Your Net Worth

By Dato' Sayed Alfeizal Sayed Ahmad and Datin Shomiriza Shomidan
Entrepreneur, Malaysia

"The new form of networking is not about climbing a ladder to success; it's about collaboration, co-creation, partnerships, and long-term value-based relationships." – Jack Hidary

The Ordinary World

I started my career as an engineer, working my way up the corporate ladder. It was a regular nine-to-five life, stable and predictable. Somehow, I took a sharp turn along the way and ended up pursuing my passion for nurturing young talents in sports.

The Drama

In my youth, I participated in quite a few sports events, but it was only when I started working that I began to acquaint myself with the other side of sports: event management. Tennis was the sport I was most familiar with, so it was no surprise that it was where my journey started. Things fell into place from there, and given my success in building the local tennis association, invitations from other sports clubs came pouring in, among them being the shooting association, badminton, cycling, flying and of course, motorsports.

I was involved with organizing tournaments and activities for these clubs until I reached a point of no return. I was invited to organize an international go-kart race in Bachok, Kelantan under the auspices of Langkawi Motorsport Club (LMC). It was important enough that I was given a special letter by Malaysia's Sports Minister for release from work. Even so, my boss did not approve. I was given a warning, and to this day, I still remember his words, *"You can't have your cake and eat it too."*

So, I had to make a choice – continue with my stable and safe job as a spacecraft engineer, dutifully working my way up the corporate ladder, or take a chance on my burgeoning passion for organizing sports events. In the end, it was no choice at all. But even though I left my passion for engineering, one of the things I learned as an engineer still stuck with me – I needed structure to make this work. So, after strategizing my plan, building my resources, and expanding my network, three years after that incident, I tendered my resignation.

The decisive moment for this decision came in 2004 when I met a very talented young go-kart driver, Nabil Jeffri, when he was only 10 years old. His father, Jan Al Jeffri, asked me to manage Nabil to become a professional racing driver, and ultimately, a Formula 1 driver. To put it bluntly, go-kart racing is a very expensive sport, but it would have been such a waste if we did not help him to achieve his dream. Therefore, I took on this challenge because I believed in him, and I thought that, even without money, we had enough resources to make it happen.

I started following him for local and international races including in India, Philippines, Macau, and Indonesia. It was worth it. Nabil was crowned as the Overall Champion of the Asian Karting Championship 2004 in the Cadet category.

When the company moved to Cyberjaya in 2005, I knew that I had to make a decision. The 20 days leave allocated to me were not enough anymore. I chose to focus on Nabil.

But, it wasn't that easy. Immediately, I was out of my depth. For him to continue racing, he would need money, and to get money, he would need sponsorships.

That was when the need to network sunk in for me.

The Key Ingredients

Here's how I built my network:

First, I needed to overcome my fear of meeting people because networking is about meeting people and making connections with them. For my network, I needed to meet CEOs of companies, top officials in the ministry, even ministers. So, I started from scratch and reached out to people – first local businesses and offices, and then building on my contacts further until they expanded into big companies and government agencies. The first step is always the hardest, but it is necessary. It costs you nothing to keep reaching out because the secret is that you have nothing to lose. The worst thing they can say is *"No."*

I would identify the key people that I wanted to be in my network. This meant identifying all the related people I needed to be in contact with to grow my business and brand. Among them were the media, corporate and potential sponsors, local and international motorsports regulatory bodies, government-related agencies, as well as artwork designers and suppliers. I always made sure that I had a "win-win" relationship with them by being willing to give, to connect, and to share with them. This way, I made friends, not just contacts.

You need to make people want to be in your network. How? Commitment to excellence is key. People look for value. So, when they get more value from you, they will engage with you. People value you based on what you are able to deliver. When people know my capability and credibility, they will seek me out to organize their events.

The sponsors want to know that they are giving money or resources to the right people, people who will deliver on what they've promised. I managed to secure the sponsorship of 150 boxes of Dunlop Tennis Balls (worth RM144,000 – US$36,000) for the Laen Tennis Association of Malaysia (LTAM) for two years because of my credibility in branding for the event and sponsor. Building your network is like filling your bus with the right people. When you deliver value, the right people will fit in the seats in your "bus" inadvertently.

Integrity is also key to having a good network because integrity translates into trust. Don't oversell, always keep promises, and always deliver more than required. When you deliver integrity, you will also connect with people who have integrity.

Never take for granted that your network will know everything that you do. Make sure to follow up and update them with your latest project and your latest contact that would be of value to them. Keep them in the loop for your success stories. That will build your credibility in their eyes.

One significant story in which the power of network has helped me was when I managed to help a talented young driver, Kasma Danial, to achieve podium in the Yamaha Yamaha 135 Super Series. He was a talented young rider who started in pocket bike racing at 10 years old. He won the Malaysian Minibike Championship 2012 (Formula KBS). In order to compete in the AAM Petronas Malaysian Cub Prix Championship, he needed to be at least 13 and above to get a racing license. However, as a very talented rider, waiting one more year before he could start racing at this level would have been a waste of his time and talent. So, using my network, I managed to make an appeal to AAM to allow him to race in that category, and he got in. He finished second place in his first race and completed second overall in the championship.

The best way to sell is by sharing the value that you offer to your network. Nowadays, with social media, it is even easier than before to share and update your network about your successes. I always make sure to share on social media the updates of my business ventures as well as updates of the talents that I manage. Not only that, you can always share your struggles too so that people can connect with you. Sometimes support comes from your network in this way too.

In my business, the media helps very much to highlight the successes of my young talents. I consider the media as one of my biggest network keys, therefore, I always invest extra time and resources to my friends in the media. I make sure to connect with them from time to time, even though there is nothing that I can update them with.

But all of this is meaningless without a vision to pursue or a goal to work towards.

My goal is to help young talents in sports to achieve their dreams. Money and resources should not hinder these young talents from achieving their dreams and make the country proud. What I can do is provide a platform to connect them with brands and companies to help them grow through the network that I've built.

I decided to put my experience organizing sports events in Langkawi to good use. I organized go-kart races and expanded into other motorsports events such as pocket bikes, bikes, drifts, and drag.

I also started businesses related to sports events, such as supplying t-shirts, corporate shirts, banners and streamers, medals and trophies, etc. Most of these suppliers still remain as my main suppliers to this day.

Gradually, I built a reputation for my company, and we were offered management of a go-kart circuit in Subang Jaya in 2008. This opportunity secured my company's position in the motorsports industry as we were now able to organize races and events at our own track.

But things weren't always easy.

In 2011, Nabil finished third overall in the Formula BMW Asia leading to Petronas discontinuing the Petronas Formula Experience (PFX) program. Nabil was left without a sponsor and almost had to stop racing altogether for the 2012 season.

It was then I decided to turn this around. If playing it safe meant sitting out an entire season, then I had to up my game. Instead of depending on local teams and sponsors, I contacted a Eurointernational team, a European team that has produced a few Formula 1 drivers in the past. I developed a brand campaign for Nabil, and they decided to take him as their main driver. I had to use my own savings and borrowed from others to keep Nabil on the team. I did that because I believed in him, his talents, and above all, his dreams. I then started to build his brand internationally as well as to attract potential sponsors.

This move was crucial. It determined whether we would continue to be on the racing team or not. He proved my faith in him was justified when he then started to set records for fastest lap times, win races, and all this eventually led to the championship. After people saw his talent, sponsors started to come pouring in. On top of that, we managed to convince a few companies to sponsor him and appoint him as their brand ambassador, like Prudential BSN Takaful that offered sponsorship for 2012 and was willing to support him until 2014.

Upon seeing Nabil's success moving up from one racing category to the other, I was inspired to help others. The connections and network I built while helping create a brand for Nabil and securing sponsorships for him opened my eyes to see that what I did for Nabil could also be done for other young talents.

In pocket bike racing, I've helped support the likes of Hafizh Syahrin (MotoGP rider) and Ramdan Rosli (Moto2) in their journey to become professional riders. Eventually, I built a reputation for myself as a manager who was genuine in helping and supporting young talents.

Parents from other sports fraternities started approaching me to manage their kids. This is how I started with Adam Arif Madzri. He has since won quite a few local and international junior golf tournaments as a representative of Malaysia, and has been offered a scholarship by the University of Texas, USA, to continue his undergraduate studies and play competitively in the NCAA Golf Division 1.

In squash, I manage Muhammad Amir Amirul Azhar (16) from Kelantan who is the winner of multiple squash competitions in both the local and international arena. He's currently ranked fifth in the World in Boys Under 17 rankings. What is inspirational about him is that despite his underprivileged background, he has tremendous talent in this sport. It would be such a waste if he was not supported.

Imran Daniel Abdul Hazli (14) is another young talent in tennis. Imran won several competitions including GD World Junior Masters (U11) in Turkey in 2015. Imran finished in the top 16 out of 250 top players around the world in the Orange Bowl 2017 (U12).

Qabil Irfan Azlan is another talent on my team. This seven-year-old boy from Terengganu has been winning pocket bike races in both his own category and in open class. Qabil represents the potential of Malaysian MotoGP riders in the future.

From his prodigious start to a somewhat rocky middle, Nabil has made a leap in progress, finishing sixth place out of 72 top drivers from more than 50 countries in World Rotax Max Challenge 2009 (go-kart) held in Sharm El Sheikh, Egypt. He was also extended an offer by Tan Sri Tony Fernandes to be part of the AirAsia ASEAN Driver Development Program and race in Formula BMW Asia 2010 where he finished fifth overall. In the same year, Nabil was awarded the National Youth Icon of Malaysia by the Minister of Sports of Malaysia. He also became the youngest Formula 1 test driver with Team Lotus in 2010 where he did an aero test of a Lotus T127 at the Imperial War Museum runway in Duxford, England.

In 2016, I was conferred the award "Darjah Indera Mahkota Pahang" by the Sultan of Pahang which enables me to use the title "Dato" before my name. This was due to my contribution to Malaysian sports community. It is a great honor indeed.

Now my business has expanded beyond motorsports to also include managing and organizing sports events such as tennis, cycling, running, and many more.

To top it all, I have managed to travel to more than 30 countries all over the world. My network has grown from just a local sports network to an international sports network spanning the globe. I am also glad that I have built a business that is about giving value to people and to society.

The business of building young talent is still new in Malaysia. I am planning a large-scale program to identify and promote young Malaysian talent in sports. I am also helping to turn them into professional athletes with their own six-figure income as well. With the network that I have, this is definitely possible.

The Wisdom

Building a network requires time and patience. It is not an overnight effort. However, with enough perseverance, you will reap the rewards multifold. And even if those partnerships do not work out in the long run, you should never burn your bridges because you will never know when you might need their help or support later.

> *"With a network, you can do twice the work in half the time."* – Sayed Alfeizal

Discipline, Hard Work & Determination.

If you have a business, networking is a lifeline to your success. Networking is the fuel that accelerates success no matter which profession you are in.

> *"The new form of networking is not about climbing a ladder to success; it's about collaboration, co-creation, partnerships, and long-term values-based relationships."* – Jack Hidary

I especially like this quote because it captures the essence of how I have built my business, which is through networking. Having good rapport with my clients, sponsors, and other related bodies have proven to be worthwhile over time. You can never go wrong by investing your time to build your network and to gain their trust by delivering your services with credibility and integrity. You would not only gain a legion of supporters but also would be able to expand your business through this network of yours.

Success Actions

Here are three success actions that you can take right now to make things happen in your business:

1. Strategize your business by getting the correct network. Identify who are the people that you need to have in your business - suppliers, clients, supporters, etc. Make a list. Then use a systematic approach to build your network.

    a. List the ways to initiate and engage with your network, and the frequency you need to be in touch with them.

    b. List the events, media engagement, and social media that you need to build your network and make time for them.

2. Ask yourself what value do I bring to my network and to my business? This is a very important question to set your credibility. It is a question on integrity. As there are hundreds of businesses out there, what will make you stand out is the value that you bring on board to the business that you do?

3. Make everyone important. In business, we deal with humans. Like it or not, we are social beings who like to feel that we are important. Make people feel important not by sucking up to them, but by connecting with them and showing them that they matter. Share your network with them too and help them win! You will never lose when you help other people win. This is how you build a long-lasting network that goes beyond business.

Go for your dreams,

Sayed & Shomi

About Author

Sayed Alfeizal Sayed Ahmad
Entrepreneur, Malaysia

An engineer by profession, Sayed Alfeizal left the rat race to pursue his passion to build and nurture young talent in sports. Among the sports talents he has helped develop in motorsports are Nabil Jeffri, F2 racecar driver; Hafizh Syahrin, a MotoGP rider; and Kasma Danial, a Moto2 rider. In tennis, there is Imran Daniel Abdul Hazli; in golf, Adam Arif Madzri; and in squash, Muhammad Amir Amirul Azhar who is currently fifth in the World Squash Ranking (U17).

He believes the power of networking has helped him create his success and the success of the young talents under him.

Contacts

- **Business Name:** Sayed Alfeizal Sayed Ahmad
- **Email:** mailto:sayedalfeizal@gmail.com
- **Facebook:** https://www.facebook.com/sayedalfeizal
- **Instagram:** https://www.instagram.com/sayedalfeizal
- **LinkedIn:** https://my.linkedin.com/in/sayedalfeizal
- **Products/Services**:
    - Organizing sports events (motorsports races, running, cycling, tennis);
    - Providing high-quality PA System services;
    - Video coverage for events and transmitted live via *YouTube* and *Facebook*;
    - Supplies of sports merchandise such as t-shirts, medals, and trophies.
    - Printing materials like banners, streamers, and backdrops.
    - Book: Porter Gale, Your Network Is Your Net Worth: Unlock the Hidden Power of Connections for Wealth, Success, and Happiness in the Digital Age

Ideal Clients:
- Corporate sectors and government agencies - to organize events for them;
- Young talents in sports - to connect them with potential sponsors to help them achieve their dreams.

- **Facebook Page for All Readers and Fans:** (Tips, Strategies, Ideas, Inspiring Stories to Make Money Fast In Business) https://www.facebook.com/groups/makemoneyfastinbusiness/, or search for "Make Money Fast in Business"

Mindset, SoulSet, and "Educashun" in the Pursuit of Wealth and Happiness.

By Silas J. Lees
Entrepreneur, UK

"Our deepest fear is not that we are inadequate. Our deepest fear is that we are powerful beyond measure. It is our light, not our darkness that most frightens us. We ask ourselves, Who am I to be brilliant, gorgeous, talented, fabulous? Actually, who are you not to be? You are a child of God. Your playing small does not serve the world. There is nothing enlightened about shrinking so that other people won't feel insecure around you. We are all meant to shine, as children do. We were born to make manifest the glory of God that is within us. It's not just in some of us; it's in everyone. And as we let our own light shine, we unconsciously give other people permission to do the same. As we are liberated from our own fear, our presence automatically liberates others." – Marianne Williamson: *A Return to Love.*

If you're like most readers, you'll have a keen interest in personal development. *"Get your mindset right, and the results will follow"* has been the mantra of the industry, and many of us have spent a lot of time, effort, and money in following the guidance of gurus in pursuit of our goals and dreams.

True, it's difficult to achieve any success in life if our mind is constantly whispering negatively to us, or continually reminding with us our limitations; after all, it knows us more intimately than anyone. It especially knows which buttons to press to prevent us from taking action. This is all in the name of trying to keep us safe.

Our minds have been programmed for survival for thousands of years; therefore, it is constantly on the lookout for danger. This is helpful when we are facing a saber-toothed tiger but not so great when we want to deliver a speech or impress a member of the opposite sex! Taking some time to make peace with our mind is a necessary step in our life journey so that it doesn't constantly sabotage our progress along the way.

Unfortunately, this is where the guidance from a lot of gurus ends, and that can be frustrating if you've tried a variety of techniques and nothing seems to work. I'd like to introduce you to another path to help in the manifestation of your dreams and desires – that of "SoulSet."

My Journey

If I may indulge you by sharing my own journey on the road to success, I hope it will lead you to an understanding of what I mean by "SoulSet." From an early age, I was always very ambitious and had big dreams of becoming the next Richard Branson.

However, my father didn't think I had the necessary skill set to be a businessman (I was very empathetic and emotional as a child), and so did his best to quash these dreams and suggested I choose of an alternative "to fall back on." I worked incredibly hard gaining my degree part-time while working full-time and then studying to become a Chartered Surveyor while also converting a barn at the same time. I passed my exams and set out in pursuit of my entrepreneurial dreams at the tender age of 28.

My first foray into business was building a property portfolio by buying my first property in December 2007, approximately 24 hours before the credit-crunch recession set in! Not to be put off, I continued buying properties which was incredibly tough as there was limited finance available, yet I didn't allow that to stop me. I was determined and used my bull-headed mindset to overcome the obstacles. Due to my achievements, I was invited to speak, mentor, and coach on behalf of the Robert Kiyosaki Rich Dad organization to help other people in building their own portfolio.

Things were going great when I met someone with whom I fell in love. My dreams of "happy-ever-after" seemed to finally be in sight. I was enjoying life immensely.

Then disaster struck!

The girl I was madly in love with admitted to seeing someone else. I was devastated! I'll be honest; I came close to ending my life over it as I couldn't believe what had happened. It seemed we were so in love. Someone whom I trusted implicitly had done the unthinkable. But, after some tears and dealing with the heartbreak, it brought out the fighter in me. Thinking *I'll show you what a mistake you've made!,* I set out with renewed enthusiasm to expand my business empire starting three new businesses, buying properties to renovate, and working 18 hours a day, seven days a week fueled by caffeine, sugar, and alcohol. It only took just over 15 months until I was physically, emotionally, mentally, and spiritually exhausted. I just gave up and retreated to my bed with an intense sense of apathy about life, wondering what was really the point of being here at all.

The Awakening

Can relate to the journey so far – doing everything that society and our peers tell us to do, only to end up unhappy and wondering if it's all worth it? For about four months, I literally couldn't get out of bed and lived off Guinness, Netflix, and Domino's Pizza while I wallowed in intense apathy. I had no drive to do anything and literally felt the will to live slipping away. Fortunately, I had the sense to reach out to a good friend of mine who suggested I get some Cognitive Behavioral Therapy, which helped enormously to expose the defective undercurrent of fallacious thinking which had undermined my progress. I thought I had my mindset right, but clearly, I was way off. I had sabotaged myself and didn't even know it.

Once I understood my thinking patterns, I experienced a synchronistic moment where I went on a three-day Ayahuasca retreat which was intensely powerful and very revealing for me. I have heard that people can have a variety of experiences when taking the powerful psychoactive brew which is featured in the retreat, so I am not recommending it here. Fortunately, my experience was out-of-this-world amazing, and it made me realize that there was a part of my human experience that I had inadvertently neglected as I got caught up in pursuing the Western dream.

That part was my soul.

During the retreat, I came face to face with how incredibly powerful our soul really is. It is the still voice that we cannot usually hear above the noise our mind constantly makes. Our mind speaks in a language which we understand, whereas our soul speaks in feelings. My soul was screaming at me, but I could not hear it, so it is no surprise that I went down a path leading to destruction.

The good news is, like the phoenix rising from the ashes, it revealed so much about me, and there is no doubt in my mind that I wouldn't have been able to learn this any other way than how it unfolded. If you are going through dark times now, or have been previously, accept that even these are taking you to a better place if you will learn to listen to the magic taking place within you. I am now deeply grateful for the young lady who was the trigger-event for all of this unfolding in my life. I can see that God does indeed work in mysterious ways and always for our benefit no matter what we might be experiencing at the time.

What is "SoulSet"?

"SoulSet" is learning to be guided by your soul on your life journey. For me, SoulSet trumps mindset by a factor of ten. It's fashionable for people to claim to be spiritual, yet they are usually so far out of tune with the true essence of who they are as to be untrue. The soul resides in all of us, and as such, we are all here on this realm to live out a purpose.

What that purpose is, is different for everyone, and it doesn't have to be in the form of huge, grand gestures or the saving of humanity. Sometimes the simpler things in life, like remembering our p's and q's, can lead us to a life of great satisfaction and contribute to others in a way that we cannot even begin to fathom.

I was recently enjoying a deep, esoteric conversation with a great friend of mine on holiday in Los Angeles when he asked me, *"Why are you so f*cking nice all the time?"* I was shocked by the question so had to ask him what he meant. He replied, "Look at what you've just done. The waitress has brought us our beers, and you said, 'Thank you so much' and I just said 'cheers!' Why do you need to be so over-the-top nice with everyone?"

The question stumped me and got me thinking for weeks afterward. Was I the ultimate people-pleaser? That answer didn't feel right. A few weeks later, I realized that I know what it's like to feel completely down on my luck and as though you're completely unacknowledged by the world around you. We never know what someone is going through, so I have always tried to engage others with a spirit of cheerful demeanor and take an interest in them, rather than what they can do for me or what I can get from them. It makes the world a better place. I also believe in karma – send out good, and good shall return to you. This, at its essence, is what I believe SoulSet is really all about.

The right mindset will assist in overcoming obstacles, fears, and insecurities in spite of our mind protesting to the contrary. With SoulSet, once you get this bit right, you realize there is very little to fear, and the world is actually quite a magical and supportive place when you learn to flow with it. What I learned on my journey through awakening is that life flows pretty effortlessly if we just allow it to.

Look at nature for example; trees, plants, vegetation, and animals reproduce and grow effortlessly without any man-made intervention. Moreover, everything within the natural eco-system of life exists to serve everything else. Think of the natural hierarchy within the animal kingdom and how abundant life is. A fruit tree doesn't produce one piece of fruit every year containing one seed. It produces abundantly, with many seeds, to ensure an abundant continuation of its species. In the raw state of nature, everything serves one another, and a natural equilibrium is established over time.

This might seem like a convoluted path I am taking you on with regards to wealth, however, the astute among you will note where I am going with this. For those who haven't grasped the immediate concept, the seeds planted within your fertile imagination will eventually germinate and give you the insight you seek. Should you wish to explore SoulSet further, I recommend reading the book *Love Is The New Religion* which intertwines higher spiritual wisdom within the narrative of the story. Then, you can see how to apply this in real life and grasp the principles at a deeper level. Head over to www.LoveIsTheNewReligion.com to find out more.

By putting SoulSet first, you evolve into the understanding that no matter what happens to you, you will see it as life serving you rather than working against you. If you can find your way into this place, the "stresses" of everyday life take on new meaning which is a beautiful place to live in. You will recognize that you are being gently guided on your path by a higher power, and so by surrendering to its wisdom, you will find life becomes more enjoyable and effortless rather than stressful. For more information, read *The Surrender Experiment* by Michael A. Singer.

"Educashun"

Most people I know didn't enjoy school, and the majority of people who leave school or university never take steps to educate themselves further during their adult lives. I would like to see the statistics for the ratio of the size of people's televisions to their personal libraries! Although as Winston Churchill famously said,

> *"The only statistics you can rely upon are the ones you falsified yourself!"*

My point is if you want to do something different in your life to create wealth, it is highly likely that you will need to educate yourself on how to do so.

I personally love reading. I mean, think about it. You can obtain a lifetime of someone's knowledge via a book that costs less than the price of the main meal in a decent restaurant! Talk about a return on investment! Sometimes, that education comes in the form of a seminar, mentor, or coach and the cost can be considerably higher. However, education has been the best investment I have made and far more entertaining than watching reality TV shows – which I presume people only watch because they don't push the boundaries of their lives and see what is actually possible to achieve in the time we have available to us on this Earth.

You can invest in yourself and see a return on that many times over the course of your lifetime. I invested £25,000 in learning how to invest in property. This has education which has paid for itself many times over, brought me greater confidence, and has given me a skill set which I can use anywhere in the world to make money. Talk about a return on investment!

In summary, I encourage you to go after your goals and dreams, and if you have no idea how to, get some "educashun" behind you, then make it happen. You'll learn either way, from the school of hard knocks (which could potentially be very costly) or by getting some support from someone with experience.

Pulling it All Together

So, do you want to create wealth in your life? Good! I actively encourage you to go for it, and I believe that you can achieve it. So, what's stopping you? You're not sure how? Okay, let me give you a few more hints and tips.

Getting your mindset right and dismissing the negative chatter is a good step and one that you will read about in countless books. I recommend books by Jim Rohn and Zig Ziglar as great places to start. I encourage you to dig deeper and get in touch with that unexplored part of you that is your soul. Your soul is ephemeral and a spark of the Divine, the Eternal and Everlasting. It's the bit you see in someone when you look deeply into their eyes, and you feel a connection. That is because we are all energetically connected, just as is all of nature.

From this place, you will realize that the only true way to create wealth and happiness is by making a contribution to others. The shining examples of entrepreneurs are those who have contributed most to humanity. I truly believe that Steve Jobs left this realm having "made a dent in the universe" – a truly noble goal to achieve within his lifetime.

When you are standing in a place of your own true power, your SoulSet, you will realize that you are limitless and able to create whatever you wish to bring to this world. I started my first job as an estate agent nearly 22 years ago. At the time, houses were still largely sold in the same way as they had been for hundreds of years. Yet with the advent of modern technology, things are about to be disrupted and changed forever.

My main goal is to revolutionize the UK property market to make selling homes as easy as checking into a hotel. It seemed like a daunting task when I started this journey three years ago, and thankfully I have persevered. We're always looking for likeminded souls to join the revolution, so head over to www.WiggyWam.com and get in touch!

Since I finally understood the power of who we all are at the core, I have to say that life has become a lot less stressful. There is little striving toward success and more a case of attracting it by virtue of who I have become. I think this is the primary reason why the Law of Attraction doesn't work for so many people – instead of drawing things to them, people inadvertently end up pushing them away. I now get to live a pretty relaxed life in the UK, which in spite being full of much bigger challenges than I have ever faced before, I am far more certain of the outcome working to my advantage and assisting me on my journey through life. I get to operate from a place of truth and inner knowing rather than from left-brained logic and subsequent heartaches when things don't work out as we expected!

> *"Never, never, never, never, never in nothing great or small, large or petty, never give in, except to convictions of honor and good sense. Never yield to force; never yield to the apparently overwhelming might of the enemy."* Winston Churchill.

I truly believe that each and every one of you reading this can achieve your goals and dreams if you have the courage to pursue them, stand in your own true power, and follow the guidance of Winston Churchill above. It will allow life to lead you effortlessly to your true calling.

Success Actions

1. Dream big dreams and make a bold decision on what you want to contribute to the world;
2. Read *Love Is the New Religion* and *The Surrender Experiment* to understand SoulSet;
3. Buy and read three books on that which you wish to contribute to the world, attend a training course, and/or find a mentor to assist you. Take daily actions towards your dreams.

Love and light always,

About the Author

Silas J. Lees
Entrepreneur, UK

Silas J. Lees is a "recovering entrepreneur" within the property industry. Having educated thousands of people on how to start buying property while building a property portfolio himself, Silas experienced a transformative spiritual awakening in 2015 which set him on a different path in life.

His awakening led to him authoring the book Love *Is The New Religion* which contains higher spiritual truths interwoven within the narrative of the compelling story offering an alternative path for humanity to follow in today's world.

Silas recently stepped into a different arena through the development of a smartphone app aimed at the property market with the intention of ultimately revolutionizing the way properties are bought, sold and rented in the UK. His aim is to make selling homes as effortless as checking into a hotel.

Silas lives in Ironbridge, Shropshire, UK which has the claim-to-fame of being the birthplace of the Industrial Revolution. You will no doubt find him enjoying his daily walks in the Shropshire countryside with his dog Neo which provides invaluable soul-recharging time through being immersed in the beauty of nature.

Contacts

- **Business Name:** WiggyWam Limited & Love Is The New Religion
- **Website:** www.wiggywam.com & www.loveisthenewreligion.com
- **Email:** love@loveisthenewreligion.com
- **Facebook:** Silas J. Lees (https://www.facebook.com/silas.leesmrics)
- **Instagram:** Silas_j._lees (https://www.instagram.com/silas_j._lees/)
- **Linked In:** https://www.linkedin.com/in/silas-j-lees-08151b142/
- **My Products/Services:** My book, Love Is The New Religion, is available to all at an affordable price and intertwines higher spiritual truths within the narrative of the story.
- **Ideal Clients: I** offer highly exclusive spiritual coaching and mentoring to entrepreneurs who have achieved a level of success yet still feel as though something is missing from their lives. I help them make the connection between that of achievement versus Divine truth.

- **Facebook Page for All Readers and Fans:** (Tips, Strategies, Ideas, Inspiring Stories to Make Money Fast In Business) https://www.facebook.com/groups/makemoneyfastinbusiness/, or search for "Make Money Fast in Business"

Mindset and Role-Model Marketing

By Tyson Sharpe
Emotional Fitness Coach, Australia

"You only achieve in life what you conquer within" – Tyson Sharpe

The Ordinary World

I was sitting in my tiny room – eight-foot by 16-foot. No. this wasn't my bedroom; this was my whole place.

I've never felt anything like it. I was happy every day living in a new country, traveling around, and making new friends. Yet, I was struck with this gut-wrenching emotion of shame and embarrassment. I found myself working as a dishwasher in a local Mexican restaurant in Toronto, Canada, living in a room that didn't have a kitchen, and the biggest challenge I was facing was the mice in the walls scratching holes through to my room.

How did I get here, you ask? Like most people, graduating from university left me with nothing more than the feeling of confusion along with a lot of debt. So, after studying psychology for six years, I left my family and loved ones to go on a two-year trip to Canada. It is true, part of me wanted to travel, feel free, and do what I wanted before I got tied down, but another side of me, however, was terrified. No, it's not because I was leaving my mom's cooking. I was running from the scary decision of what I wanted to do for a career. Every time a friend would ask me about my studies and ask if I wanted to be a psychologist, a part of me would cringe.

Have you ever felt so stuck that each time you revisited the problem, you felt the finger-trap tighten? That's how I felt whenever the topic of a future career was brought up.

One day after finishing a 10-hour shift, I found the mice had triumphantly worked their way through the wall into my room once again. It was in that moment the finger-trap snapped.

The Turning Point

My personal development journey was born out of sheer pain and worry for my future. Since I didn't know what to do, I did anything! I found the book *How To Win Friends and Influence People* and started flicking pages. For some odd reason, applying the simple relationship tools learned in that book set a fire in my belly to know more.

I soon started reading anything I could get my hands on relating to the topics of success, psychology, wealth, and happiness. I even emailed Dr. Phil and his team for advice on how to help people on stage! And, yes, I'm still waiting for his reply.

I finally felt as though I was on a path. I was building deeper relationships, was being promoted several times in my job, earning more money, and started to be known as "the smart guy."

Despite the progress, I still had no clue which direction my path was going until I came across the world of coaching.

I found a video on *YouTube* of the great man Tony Robbins coaching a woman through her depression. This wasn't a normal therapy session. This was in front of 3,000 people as he instructed her to get <u>more</u> depressed! Could this man be insane? Or maybe just insensitive?

It turns out, it was the perfect exercise for the woman to learn something about herself. Tony was less concerned about <u>why</u> she was depressed and more focused on <u>how she expresses</u> depression. He was able to help her see which internal patterns drive her depression, why unconsciously she was addicted to the pattern, and options of how to create a shift in a heartbeat.

I have never cried so much in my life! Seeing her move from worry and fear to total freedom in the matter of one conversation was a miracle. Which superpowers did Tony Robbins possess? Was this a placebo? Maybe it was a one-off case?

Whatever the answer was, I had to find out! When I saw Tony had an online coaching course teaching all his strategies, tools, and tactics, jumping in was a must!

There was one hurdle. The investment for the program was half of everything I had in the bank. Have you ever felt fear grab you by the gut and not let go? This was my experience. Every part of me wanted to curl up and shy away from the uncertainty.

However, in those moments of fear, I also realized I had similar patterns to the lady in the Robbins' intervention. Her patterns of depression were helping her avoid a deeper, more scary decision. I too had my patterns of comfort, as I avoided the decision to move forward with my career.

I had been shying away from my dreams, goals, and aspirations because I didn't want to feel uncomfortable. Well, I was now on the edge of a cliff, trying to peek over to see if there was a safe landing. What did I do? I decided to take five steps back from the cliff, take a deep breath, summon all the courage I could muster, and take a massive leap into the uncertainty.

I jumped into the program, and what I learned from it changed my life forever!

The Vision

Just like the women in the intervention video, I learned that human behavior and the emotional patterns we experience are not as they seem on the surface. There are many unconscious side-benefits to the patterns we develop, and once you understand them, you can make a shift to not only achieve any result you want but live a rich and fulfilling life on the journey.

Despite at the time being in beautiful Banff, Alberta, surrounded by mountains and wildlife, I was locked in my room writing down word for word whatever came out of Tony's mouth. I became obsessed with learning and practicing the skills and tools necessary to rapidly change someone's life. It's fair to say I learned more in 1 week on how to accomplish this than in six years of university.

Yes, I had found my path!

Equipped with this knowledge, I made a massive decision to move back to my hometown of Melbourne, Australia, to start my own coaching business. As I did, I made a commitment to myself, no matter what internal or external challenges were in my way, I would succeed to help others increase their level of success and fulfillment in their lives.

This would soon be tested.

The Call to Action

Fueled with energy, motivation, excitement, and passion, I opened my laptop, bought a domain name, and announced to the world that I was becoming a life coach. Not a day that went by where I wasn't working on my business. I was using all the tools under the sun! I used social media, email marketing, *Facebook* ads, blogs, eBooks, webinars – you name it, I used it.

I was spreading the word on how to feel happier, how to live a fulfilling life, and how to overcome any challenge in your life! This was life-transforming information, I thought. Didn't they know how beneficial an improved mindset can be? I thought after sharing what I had learned, my calendar would be booked with clients within weeks.

I was in for a shocking realization.

The Downfall

Despite the hustle and grind, a positive attitude, optimistic outlook, and a smile on my face, I had very little business results to show for it. In fact, after nine months of working non-stop, I had zero clients.

I was left feeling stuck, helpless, and lost. Maybe I wasn't good enough. Maybe successful people had a special gift that I didn't. What was I doing wrong? Were my tools and strategies all a lie? Was I just a fake and a phony?

Intense shame and embarrassment started to surface yet again.

The Key Ingredients

In the pit of despair, one thought kept my hopes alive. Could it be that my external results were being driven by an internal pattern? If so, this is well within my control.

You have probably heard the *saying "There are no business problems, just personal problems being amplified in your business."* This statement was true for me. What was this internal pattern holding me back? Could it simply be outside my own conscious awareness? How do I find out?

I decided to take the advice I was preaching to other people for months. I hired my own coach. Only once I took this step could I explore my own mind and find the internal tweaks that needed to be made.

While exploring the depths of my mind, my coach helped me see I was like a fly banging my head against the window, trying to get to the garden. I simply couldn't see the glass wall in front of me. These internal patterns were holding me back from the level of freedom, income, and impact I knew I could achieve.

What was that wall?

Identity

What I learned during this period was shocking, and it revealed to me why so many business owners remain stuck and never break through, regardless of the level of hustle or how many strategies they try. Science has now shown that 95% of all your decisions and actions are unconscious. Therefore, your results may be driven by a strong undercurrent that's outside your awareness. What pulls this undercurrent more than anything? It's your internal identity.

The strongest force within you right now is your need to remain consistent with how you see yourself. Because I had the identity of a new coach who needed to prove myself, my brain would always self-sabotage my performance to remain consistent with that identity. If you're like most business owners, you may be looking to achieve a new result so you can become someone new. In reality, before you achieve any new external result, you must make the necessary shifts to your current internal identity.

When you shift your identity first, you become the version of yourself capable of overcoming the challenges necessary to achieve the result.

The "Circumstance Dance"

This is where you avoid the trap I call the "circumstance dance."This is where business owners make decisions and take actions based on their current circumstances, like, for example, the amount of money, time, energy, or resources you currently possess. I'm sure you can see, however, that your past decisions and actions have led you to the results you now see in front of you. These results are your current reality. Therefore, if you make decisions based on your current circumstances, you will always achieve what you've always gotten.

If you are to break through to new results for your online business, you must make decisions and take actions based on who you need to <u>become</u>, and what's possible in your future.

Safe Problem

One thing you may have already realized is that underneath all human behavior and emotion lies a deep fear that if we are not enough, we won't be worthy of love. This is a deep unconscious fear that plays its role in your entrepreneurial journey and may be holding you back, even if you're not aware of it.

If you're like most people, the one thing that triggers your deepest fear more than anything is failure. Therefore, to remain safe, your brain creates "safe problems" to distract you from any decision or action that may lead to failure.

Have you ever wondered why your brain defaults to the patterns of doubt, worry, anxiety, and confusion when times get uncertain? Ever wondered why procrastination, distraction, and hesitation are so prominent within the entrepreneurial journey?

Your brain has learned unconsciously that these patterns keep you safe from failure and therefore facing your deepest fear of not being good enough. If you have been in business for any length of time, you may see the irony here.

Getting outside your comfort zone, spreading your message, and failing while reiterating ideas are all core ingredients for entrepreneurial success! As you can see, this is also a challenge and a "problem." However, it's a problem that requires a risk that leads to deeper levels of growth and contribution.

You will always have challenges in your life. The beautiful aspect of this is that you get to choose your challenges. Do you want to be mired down with the challenges that keep you stuck in a comfort zone? Or do you want to call upon more of yourself, face your true, deepest fears, and tackle challenges that lead to deeper levels of growth and contribution?

The Growth

To become the coach capable of inspiring new results, I needed to shift my identity, start making decisions based on who I need to become, and choose to tackle quality problems. How would I do that?

I started paying very close attention to my thoughts. I made it a habit every morning to place on paper all the sentences that were flying through my mind, making sure I was completely aware of any hidden limiting beliefs. Whenever I was feeling low or stuck in a rut, thought-journaling allowed me to observe the thoughts I was believing and give me the opportunity to separate myself from them.

Because my thoughts were now in check, it left space for me to manage my emotional world. I found myself empowered by the exercise of choosing which emotional state I wanted to feel throughout the day. If I had coaching sessions all day, I was able to channel a more calm, insightful, and wise side of me. On the other hand, if I had a scary task outside my comfort zone, I managed to effectively summon the courage, discipline, and focus to follow through.

This means the action I was taking regularly was very efficient and deliberate. Scheduling and planning became a true strength, and sticking to the tasks I had set were non-negotiable. With new action came new beliefs. I started reminding myself how powerful my coaching program was. I knew I was the type of coach that creates miracles in people's lives. Instead of fixating on the income generated by signing up a new client, my mind was now anchored towards how I can serve, the difference I can make, and how my client's investment would be made back 10 times!

My identity had now shifted. I was a successful coach!

The Reward

My unconscious mind was now working for me instead of against me. It seemed I would follow through on anything scary and uncertain if it meant holding the identity of a successful coach. After making the internal shifts necessary, I landed seven new, paying clients in just one week.

I was doing backflips with excitement!

Where could this now take me? What's possible from here if the necessary internal shifts I need to make are within my control? I was now seeking the opportunity for my next big jump.

That opportunity came when I was introduced to a coach that was absolutely crushing it. He was already making multiple, six-figures and now scaling to the million-dollar mark. His *Facebook* page was covered with celebrity branding, he had a published book, an online program, and had raving fans attending in-person events.

How do I get to that level? I thought. *What is he doing differently? What are his beliefs? What's his internal identity?* I decided to reach out myself and find those answers. Once again, I found myself running into fear concerning money.

The investment for his program was AU$12K, and you guessed it, I didn't have that kind of money. The thoughts were circling in my head, *There's no way I can make that investment, I don't have the money!*. Those doubts brought up the emotions of frustration, worry, and plenty of fear. I was making decisions based on my current circumstances, and the worry presented a "safe problem" that was restricting my growth.

I decided to break out of my "circumstance dance" by thinking from a place of possibility. Despite my legs feeling like jelly and a quiver in my voice as I recited my credit card number over the phone, I made a deposit of AU$2K. This left me in the situation of needing to make AU$10K the next month to jump into the program. No, I had never made that much in a month before! Was I crazy, or was this what's necessary?

I hopped on 30 sales calls that month, and before each one, I would remind myself of what mattered most. The questions cycled in my head, *Who am I becoming? What big, bold decisions can I make? How can this quality challenge help me grow, so I have more to give?*

The results at the end of the month blew me away. I not only made my first AU$10K month, but I also donated more to charity and through random acts of kindness than ever before and recorded the entire journey to share my lessons along the way.

The results left me speechless. Yet, with the little voice I had left, I decided to teach one of my new clients the very same shift I had made.

Paul came to me because he was struggling with sales. He was selling about AU$30k in product per month in which he would make a small percentage for his income. He had a beautiful family to provide for and wanted to see what was possible for him. Paul felt lost, stuck, and hopeless in his situation.

After just three sessions, I helped Paul shift the unconscious mental patterns that were keeping him stuck, and the results were amazing! In the following two months, Paul sold AU$178K and AU$157K in product. He was more shocked than anyone and attributed his cosmic leap to nothing more than a shifted mindset.

Four months later, Paul messaged me with an update explaining that he had just broken his all-time sales goal of AU$200K in a single month.

Outstanding!

These are the changes that are possible when you remove the unconscious mental blocks that are holding you back, and you condition the version of yourself capable of your next big breakthrough.

So, where did this lead me?

I was now coaching more and more digital marketers, coaches, and online agency owners. I became obsessed with finding the answers to whatever challenges they came up against. These challenges were around messaging, choosing a niche, finding the right clients, and making enough income to stay in the positive.

As you can imagine, I started noticing some patterns. I started to realize why it can be so tough to get a business off the ground, to earn a consistent income, and reach the level of freedom that most online entrepreneurs want to achieve.

I've come to call this trap the "credibility cradle." Have you ever seen a tiny toddler try to get out of a cradle and struggle until they give up? A very similar pattern occurs with new entrepreneurs. When you don't have much credibility, it's a struggle to get clients, and because you don't have consistent clients, it's hard to build credibility. This is the trap that most online business owners find themselves in and never seem to get to the point where they become the go-to expert in their field.

I had found myself at this stage booking speaking gigs, organizing key business collaborations, and my client base was solid. How was it that I got over the hump? How did I get out of my own cradle?

The answer: "Role-Model Marketing."

Not only was I having huge breakthroughs in my business, I was making leaps and bounds in my personal life also! I took the courage, discipline, and focus I had developed and applied it to routines of fitness, health, and overall wellbeing. I was now running consistently; I successfully cut sugar and flour out of my diet and even started taking cold showers. Yes, even throughout winter.

Along with many other radical changes, I was sharing my personal transformation on my *Facebook* account. Every milestone and breakthrough resulted in massive levels of engagement. The bigger the breakthrough, the bigger the engagement.

After a few short months, I had a massive following of friends, clients, peers, and prospects all paying close attention to my journey and were inspired by my heightened level of courage and leadership.

This reach meant more prospects, business leaders, and collaboration partners were finding out who I am, how I help, and what value I can add to their business.

As I was to find out, my page offered plenty of social proof as people scrolled to view posts with 100, 200, even 300-plus pieces of engagement. Do you think these posts lead you speaking gigs, book deals, business collaborations, and partnerships? You bet!

One of the more magical opportunities that came my way was when I found myself at a business lunch with 15 other business owners. This was a high-end restaurant in which the whole upper floor was rented out overlooking the beautiful Melbourne city.

Why was I there?

The plan was for us 16 business leaders to firstly collaborate to ensure every one of our businesses was thriving before we work together to create another profitable business in partnership. I was surrounded by those 10, 15, even 20 years my senior all focused on doing what they can to make sure my business is thriving in the next 60-90 days! How was this possible?

It occurred all from the back end of being a relentless role-model. As people followed my journey, I started getting invited to business and networking events. Even the speakers at these events had recognized me from my *Facebook* posts and videos!

When you come from a place of service and contribution in those environments, people want to have you around, get to know you, and see how you can do business together. What you also may find on your journey is that the more you inspire others with your story, the more business opportunities come your way. The more opportunities that come your way, the more you can inspire with your journey.

Can you see how you have shifted from the trap of the "credibility cradle" to the snowball effect of positive momentum?

The Brightness for the Future

I now have moved forward to teaching digital marketers and online business owners on how to make the same transition. What I have found is that there is a magical blend of both mindset and business that lead to these incredible results. You must first develop the courage, discipline, focus, and determination to become a true role-model in your own life. This means following through on the tasks that are tough, facing your fears, and jumping into the unknown knowing it's required for growth.

What are the areas in your life that are scary and bring up high levels of uncertainty? What's something you can follow through on where you know, despite the risk, deeper levels of growth await you?

Once you have the mind to become a relentless role model, people will start to follow you, support you, and cheer you on. From that place, you set a level of credibility to be noticed by those prospects, peers, and mentors that offer key business opportunities to move forward.

What are the business opportunities that would move your business forward? It could be as a guest speaker, co-author, or guest blogger. Maybe you seek to organize joint ventures with influencers in your industry or collaborate with a company offering complementary services.

In a couple of short years, I have now coached over 200 business leaders one on one, helping them create the necessary changes to their mind and business to start generating AU$10-20k a month and set a platform to scale.

The Wisdom

In piecing this all together, you can probably see the components required for your next personal and business breakthrough. I think there's a reason why nine out of 10 businesses fail in any five-year period. It can be easy to think that your next breakthrough is found in a new online strategy, tool, and/or tactic. And yes, those strategies are vital! However, your real breakthrough, the type that earns you freedom, income, and impact, is the breakthrough that occurs between your ears. I would not have become a role-model if I didn't first summon the courage to take up scary challenges, go outside my comfort zone, and say *"Yes!"* to the opportunities in front of me.

Some challenges stand between you and your goals, and that's a beautiful thing. The real question is whether you have the internal resources capable of tackling the challenges consistently for your journey. If your answers are found in a business strategy, you will always be looking for a new strategy. However, if your answer is found in your strengthened, inner, mental muscles of focus, discipline, creativity, love, passion, and insight, you will have the peace of mind knowing you can break down any obstacle in your way.

> *Success is not about your resources; it's about your internal resourcefulness* – Tony Robbins

Sucess Actions

There are a set of wise questions you can ask yourself to allow your unconscious mind to start working for you instead of against you. This set of questions will allow you to tap into your identity, avoid the "circumstance dance," and focus on quality problems that allow you to grow.

1. If you already achieved the result you were after, what would you be thinking and believing? What would you believe about your business, clients, and future? What would you believe about yourself?

2. Which emotions would you be feeling most often? These are the emotional states that will provide the internal resourcefulness necessary to overcome your current challenges.

3. Which actions would you take, and what bold decisions would you make if you were thinking from possibility and not from your current circumstances?

You can now start to see there are no business problems, only personal problems being amplified in your business. You can also see that there are no challenges can't be overcome with the right level of internal resourcefulness.

To all your success and fulfillment,

Tyson

About the Author

Tyson Sharpe
Emotional Fitness Coach, Australia

Tyson Sharpe is an emotional fitness coach, helping digital marketers and online entrepreneurs break through their mental ceilings, become the authority in their market, and set a consistent client base on social media.

Contacts

Business Name: Tyson Coaching

- **Website:** https://tysoncoaching.com
- **Email:** tyson@tysoncoaching.com
- **Facebook:**
  https://www.facebook.com/tyson.sharpe.37
- **Instagram:**
  https://www.instagram.com/tysoncoaching/
- **LinkedIn:**
  https://www.linkedin.com/in/business-mindset-coach/
- **Your services:** One On One Coaching, Small Group Coaching
- **Online Course:** Business Mindset Installed
- **Ideal Clients:** Digital marketers and online entrepreneurs who have a true passion to help grow meaningful businesses.

- **Facebook Page for All Readers and Fans:** (Tips, Strategies, Ideas, Inspiring Stories to Make Money Fast In Business) https://www.facebook.com/groups/makemoneyfastinbusiness/, or search for "Make Money Fast in Business"

It All Started with a Doodle

By Yentti Amir
Teacher and "Momprenuer," Malaysia

"You cannot make people learn. You can only provide the right conditions for learning to happen." – Vince Gowmon

The Ordinary World

I grew up in Malaysia. Being an IT graduate, I was inexperienced in education, but my passion turned into a great success. I am a mom of five and very passionate about education. It all started at home when I tried to teach the Quran to my elder two. Like all my children, their focus span was limited. They couldn't sit still when we opened the book. It was quite challenging and frustrating.

I want to be the first to teach them about the Holy Book recitation. As The Prophet (ﷺ) said, *"The best among you (Muslims) are those who learn the Qur'an and teach it."* I put forward my best to deliver the Quran – we scribbled to get our hands involved and did lots of body movement. We clapped our hands and each session turned out to be a great playtime of learning. So, I decided to share the joy with all my kids in my

187

neighborhood. I then took them to a nearby kindergarten for volunteer teaching. The kids were overwhelmed, and the teachers were fascinated with the so-called innovation in teaching the Quran. The parents were impressed, too!

My success story in this tuning of the traditional Quran teaching method started to spread among adults. I decided to voluntarily train teachers in the entire state. I then took a bigger step by collaborating with a module provider. From a single state to nationwide, the teaching tools I developed were widely used in hundreds of kindergartens. This all happened within five months before we left Malaysia to so we could pursue our studies elsewhere. I was very keen to pursue my study in education while my husband was doing his Ph.D. abroad.

The Drama

In the UK, I presented my teaching kit upon applying for a university placement. I was not confident to do a master's degree in the area that I hadn't already had any basic knowledge. Surprisingly, the Head of Education was impressed with my achievement in Malaysia. I was accepted for studies in M.A. Education at my dream university.

The excitement turned into apathy after I attended the first class. Suddenly, I felt fear and doubted the dreams I'd had since childhood. I started to worry about the lengthy assignments and my husband's striving for his Ph.D. There was no family around to help look after the kids. I decided to quit and believed that was not a mistake.

The Turning Point

I felt relieved and thankful to God for guiding me in this big decision. I was back to my normal routine sending the kids off to school. One special morning, the headteacher welcomed the kids. Upon leaving school, I smiled and told her, *"I have quit!"*

She then replied, *"We are in the same boat!"*

The headteacher really made my day. From a morning greeting, it turned out to be a motivating therapy session. She considered me lucky because I quit after the first class. She actually gave it a try for six months. Our morning chat ended with great plans ahead for me to keep on reaching the stars. She guided me for an alternative learning route with less theoretic but more hands-on teaching opportunities. Being grateful, I believed that God had helped her share His plan for me to make the most out of our stay in the UK.

The Vision

I feel that I am meant to help young children develop their potential. I aim to help adults, also by teaching them how to teach in a stress-free teaching environment. I believed there is a mutually enjoyable learning journey between kids and adults. A positive environment can always be created and cherished.

The Call to Action

I completed my studies and had great teaching experience in the UK. As a result, I gained a good understanding of the Early Years and National Curriculum. I always was keen to learn and put into practice all the teaching techniques I learned. With my calm and patient nature, the children responded well in the classroom. My project was recognized by the school as one of the major attributes to achieve the "Best International School" award.

I dedicated myself to Malaysian Community School on the weekends. Appointed as the principal, I led a team of volunteers to teach young children about Islam and the Quran. The weekly class turned into the kids' most-awaited event. From the volunteers to the children – everyone had so much fun learning. It was no longer a boring, sit-still, religious class with the talk-and-chalk.

After years of experience abroad, we had to return to our home country, Malaysia. There, I set up a learning center to help young children. It was successful and imprinted in the children's minds that learning is fun. I developed English modules to cater the needs of mastering English as Second Language (ESL). We had trial runs years after years.

I did not implement any marketing strategy or bombastic promotions. I only worked two hours daily and met with five different groups of children each week. My class was always full. Again, the fun learning environment started to spread mouth-to-mouth. I began to train adults as volunteers and did not have any intention turning my passion for teaching into a business opportunity.

The Downfall

Then, one day, I received a call from the company which I "shared" my ideas prior leaving for the UK. I was very excited when they called and asked for a meeting. I believe a good teaching technique must always be improved. Yes, after five years, the time had come to modify and improve upon the teaching tools I had developed for them.

Up to my surprise, the purpose of the meeting was not what I expected. The meeting was all about listening to the company's success story. From their initial failures, I helped them with my teaching pedagogy. They asked me to travel more than two hours to actually confer with them, but then they decided to discontinue my association with them. After being treated so unprofessionally, I stepped away with a broken heart. I comforted myself. There must always be a rainbow after a heavy rain.

The Key Ingredients

I possess a strong will and passion for working with young children. Back home, I started to question myself, *"How can I continue helping the children and the adults?"* Thousands of children and hundreds of teachers have never been disappointed with my teaching approach. My endless efforts were just not being appreciated by the so-called "money-machine makers," and I got so frustrated.

I comforted myself and being optimistic that God always has the best plan. I glanced through the bookshelf and saw my doodles I had done with the kids. It's our little Quran memorization project! It had all started at home two years ago after they came back from the UK. Then my doodles sparked enjoyment to these children and adults during my voluntary teaching at a couple of settings.

The Growth

I made my first move by calling a publisher. I shared my success story with the doodles. A few days later, I was then invited to present my ideas, but I wasn't prepared. I just wanted to have a go at it as a revenge to my coarse treatment bye previous company. I traveled to the presentation for more than two hours. Upon my arrival, they asked for slide presentations. I brought nothing but my little book project, but my presentation was remarkable. They believed it would be a worthy investment even though they had foreseen a risk publishing this new concept of book.

After the presentation, I got stuck for almost half a year. I was not able to submit my manuscript to the publisher. It was difficult to turn my ideas into words. I did not give up and requested to meet with the design team. It was an inspiring meeting, and I believed my ideas could be developed into a great book. I made my first step, and my husband came into the picture. Both my husband and I are now the authors. Together, we worked well, and the first book had a pre-order of more than 2,000 copies. The publisher had to reprint a second edition soon after the first one was released.

This book impressed many people, both locally and internationally. Friends and families helped sell the books, and the number of sales was outstanding. Title after title was released, and their schedule was packed with roadshows promoting these books. I also worked with my best friend compiling all their lesson plans in UK. Now, they have established a website, www.tafsirmini.com, selling the books.

It's such a blessing to attend a course by my classmate, Izdihar, at the university. Inspired by my success, I started to dream about setting up an online platform. It was just a dream for a non-business-minded person like me. One day, Izdihar contacted me to order the book which I had given him as a present!

The Reward

Being able to contribute to society through the books and the program I have developed while serving my own family of five children is the best reward that I could have ever hoped for. I am hoping to serve more people as the Prophet Muhammad (PBUH) said: *"The best among you is those who are the most beneficial to human."*

The greatest reward that I wish to get is when I can later meet see what Prophet Muhammad saw in paradise. May Allah reward m with *Jannatul Firdaus*.

The Brightness of The Future

I am working to develop an online platform to reach more parents and teachers around the globe to make learning more meaningful and fun for children. Religious education is perfect and working with children is a reflection. We reflect how we are connected to God and how much is our understanding of the Holy Book.

The Wisdom

Al-Quran contains words from the All-Mighty Allah, the Creator. The words are not only meant to be read but also understood and practiced in our daily life. As parents and educators, we must find ways to nurture fun learning in children for them to fall in love with the Quran. For example, effective storytelling will make them feel more curious and excited. Effective storytelling can provide positive impacts on children's learning such as elevating their enthusiasm to read, understand and further memorize the Quran.

The Prophet (ﷺ) said, *"The best among you (Muslims) are those who learn the Qur'an and teach it."*

Success Actions

1. Must have good intentions;
2. Must be willing to make continuous improvement;
3. Do something from your heart.

About the Author

Yentti Amir
Teacher and "Momprenuer," Malaysia

Yentti Amir is a mother of five children and a graduate in Bachelor of Information Technology from Universiti Teknologi PETRONAS. Experienced as a principle at Malaysia School of Nottingham (UK) in addition to being an Early Years Volunteer at Nottingham Nursery School and Teaching Assistant at Radford Primary School, she is also the founder of KausarXcel (Center for Holistic Learning), a training center for holistic education for children, teachers, and educators.

Contacts

- **Business Name:** TafsirMini.Com
- **Website:** www.tafsirmini.com
- **Email:** mailto:tafsirmini@gmail.com
- **Facebook:** tafsirmini
- **Instagram:** tafsirmini
- **Products/ Services:** Books and training for teachers
- **Ideal Clients:** Children, parents, and teachers

- **Facebook Page for All Readers and Fans:** (Tips, Strategies, Ideas, Inspiring Stories to Make Money Fast In Business) https://www.facebook.com/groups/makemoneyfastinbusiness/, or search for "Make Money Fast in Business"

www.ingramcontent.com/pod-product-compliance
Lightning Source LLC
Chambersburg PA
CBHW070329220526
45467CB00001B/96

*   9 7 8 1 7 0 1 9 1 7 0 9 5 *